TOFU
Cookery

25TH-ANNIVERSARY EDITION

Louise Hagler

BOOK PUBLISHING COMPANY

Summertown, Tennessee

Library of Congress Cataloging-in-Publication Data

Hagler, Louise.
    Tofu cookery / by Louise Hagler. — 25th anniversary ed.
        p. cm.
    Includes index.
    ISBN 978-1-57067-220-0
    1. Cookery (Tofu)   I. Title.

    TX814.5.T63H338 2008
    641.6'5655—dc22

                                        2007052174

Cover Photo: Enchiladas (page 69),
Sprouted Lentil Salad (page 36), and
Cheesecake with kiwi and blueberries (page 155)

Food Stylists: Jane Ayers, Louise Hagler, Barbara Jefferson
Photographers: Michael Bonnickson, Warren Jefferson, Thomas Johns
Artwork: Peter Hoyt, Gregory Lowry
Author photo: Mary Desmit
Cover and interior design: John Wincek, Rhonda Wincek
Cover photo: Warren Jefferson

Printed in Hong Kong

Book Publishing Company
P.O. Box 99
Summertown, TN 38483
888-260-8458
www.bookpubco.com

ISBN 13: 978-1-57067-220-0

17 16 15 14 13 12 11 10 09   2 3 4 5 6 7 8 9

Book Publishing Company is a member
of Green Press Initiative. We chose to print
this title on paper with postconsumer
recycled content, processed without
chlorine, which saved the following
natural resources:

62 trees

2,921 pounds of solid waste

22,751 gallons of water

5,481 pounds pounds of greenhouse gases

43 million BTUs of total energy

For more information, visit
www.greenpressinitiative.org.

*(Paper calculations from Environmental Defense
Paper Calculator: www.papercalculator.org)*

BOOK
PUBLISHING
COMPANY

green
press
INITIATIVE

Contents

Acknowledgments

This book is dedicated to the memory of our beloved community members and friends who contributed to this book:

Dorothy Bates

Stewart Butler

Dawn (Huddleston) Hendrickson

"Honey" Evelyn Tepper

Our special thanks go to the following people now or formerly part of The Farm Community in Summertown, Tennessee, for originating and developing the recipes in this book: Dorothy Bates, Stewart Butler, Beth Cramer, Mary (Felber) Flannery, Claire Fitch, Louise Hagler, Nancy (Haren) Reichlin, Starr (Sarah) Hergenrather, Dawn (Huddleston) Hendrickson, Jane Hunnicutt, Sylvia (Hupp) Diaz, Suzy Jenkins-Viavant, Roberta Kachinsky, Betsy (Keller), Marian (Lyon) Grebanier, Kate Longfellow (Kathryn McClure), Earlynn (McIntyre), Leila McClure (Cornelia Mandelstein), Lee Meltzer, Anna (Ann) Moore, Dr. Stacey (Moore) Kerr, Laurie Praskin, Carol (Pratt) Taft, Colleen Pride, Rachel (Sythe) Kai, "Honey" Evelyn Tepper, Ruth (Thomas) Morris, Lani Young

About the Author

LOUISE HAGLER is a pioneer in creating vegan cuisine with tofu and other soyfoods to satisfy the Western palate. For over thirty years, she has continued to create vegan cookbooks that present a wide variety of tasty, easy-to-prepare, familiar dishes incorporating soyfoods of all kinds.

Besides being a cookbook author, Louise is a mother and grandmother, food writer, book production supervisor, food stylist, soy technician, nutrition educator, and traveling culinary teacher. In her cooking classes, Louise showcases her quick and easy recipes, revealing special cooking tips and secrets of success for this healthful cuisine. The class menus demonstrate the amazing versatility of all kinds of soyfoods prepared in ways that are warmly welcomed into daily menus.

Louise also works with Plenty International, a not-for-profit alternative relief and development organization, as a soy technician and nutrition educator in Mexico and Guatemala. These projects introduce soyfoods as alternative protein for undernourished populations, and also seek to reintroduce native protein sources and teach organic, sustainable farming and gardening for food security. Visit www.plenty.org/index.htm for more information.

Other book titles from Louise include *Miso Cookery*, *Soyfoods Cookery*, *Lighten Up! with Louise Hagler*, *Meatless Burgers*, *Tofu Quick & Easy*, and *The Farm Vegetarian Cookbook*.

So much has come to light about the world of soybeans since this book was first put together as a project of The Farm, a vegan intentional community located in Tennessee, in the early 1970s. As of this writing, thousands of studies have been done on the various nutritional and health factors related to the soybean, the overwhelming majority with positive conclusions.

Tofu is a soyfood that has been consumed for centuries in Asian cultures, which have some of the best statistics in the world for low rates of cancer and heart disease. Soyfoods in general, and tofu in particular, are not magic remedies for any malady, nor can they alone correct an otherwise poor diet. But for most healthy people, these power-packed foods are well worth adding to their menu. With the exception of those with soy allergies, all people can benefit from two to three daily servings of soyfoods, including tofu. The recipes in this book will make that easy to do!

Today tofu hardly needs any introduction. It has truly become a household word. Many have paid tribute to this noble soyfood, despite its being the brunt of a number of jokes in the media. One fact remains: tofu is one of the most versatile protein foods in the world. Tofu, also known as bean curd, is made by curding mild, white soymilk. It is high in protein and relatively low in calories, fat, and carbohydrates. Tofu is an economical source of protein and, like all plant foods, contains no cholesterol.

Tofu originated in Asia hundreds of years ago, where it still can be found in many forms not generally seen or available in the Western hemisphere. The recipes in this book incorporate the use of tofu in ways that are recognizable to the Western palate. These are only a sampling of the culinary delights possible with tofu, ranging from the familiar to the international and exotic. Tofu can be prepared in a variety of ways and incorporated into main dishes, breads, desserts, soups, salads, salad dressings, and dips, sufficient for any meal, snack, or party.

With its growing popularity, tofu has become easy to find in supermarkets everywhere. It can also be found in the growing number of Asian food shops and natural food stores. Small tofu shops and larger processing plants have sprouted up around the country. If you become a serious tofu chef or use large amounts of tofu, you might want to make arrangements to get it right from the source; alternatively, you can make your own tofu at home.

Tofu is an excellent food for babies, children, and the elderly since it is a wholesome, complete vegetable protein that is very easy to digest. It is also a good food for sensitive stomachs. For babies, tofu can be processed in a blender or ground in a baby-food grinder with your choice of flavorings, fruits, or vegetables. Higher protein foods like tofu are generally introduced to babies when they are seven to eight months of age, after they have first been introduced to baby cereals, fruits, and vegetables. Older babies and young children enjoy small cubes of plain tofu for snacking.

The nutritional content of tofu will vary slightly depending on what variety of bean was used and what method was used to process it, but all tofu is rich in high-quality protein and is a good source of B vitamins. When tofu is curded with calcium sulfate, it also becomes a good source of calcium. Tofu is low in sodium, making it an excellent food choice for those on sodium-restricted diets.

TABLE 1 Nutritional analysis for ¼ pound (113.5 grams) tofu, traditionally prepared with calcium sulfate and magnesium chloride (nigari)

Nutrient	Firm Tofu	Soft Tofu
Calcium	228.0 mg	126.0 mg
Calories	79.45	69.24
Carbohydrates	1.92 g	2.04 g
Cholesterol	0 g	0 g
Fat	4.73 g	4.19 g
Fat, saturated	0.98 g	0.60 g
Fiber	1.02 g	0.23 g
Iron	1.82 mg	1.25 mg
Niacin	0.11 mg	0.60 mg
Potassium	168.0 mg	136.0 mg
Protein	9.30 g	7.43 g
Riboflavin	0.076 mg	0.04 mg
Sodium	13.62 mg	9.08 mg
Thiamin	0.072 mg	0.05 mg
Zinc	0.94 mg	0.72 mg

In this 25th-anniversary revised edition of *Tofu Cookery*, I have aimed to bring all the recipes up to date for today's nutritional standards. I have added many new recipes to reflect more currents tastes and trends to complement the old favorites. There is more variation in choice of sweeteners. Overall, the fat and salt in the recipes have been greatly reduced, and I've eliminated frying wherever possible or offered alternative preparation methods. For cooking oil, I suggest organic extra-virgin olive oil, or organic expeller-pressed canola oil or organic light olive oil where a milder taste is called for. For baking and frying, I have added the option of high-quality, unrefined organic coconut oil. If a strong coconut flavor is objectionable, look for organic coconut oil with the flavor removed.

In many of the uncooked recipes, such as salad dressings and dips, consider the option of adding flaxseed oil, hempseed oil, or chia seed oil. Although soybeans naturally contain omega-6 and omega-3 essential fatty acids, including these other oils adds a healthful boost.

As you gain experience using tofu, you can adapt many of your own favorite recipes to include it. Many of the recipes in this book were adapted from old family favorites when The Farm was pioneering a vegan, soy-based diet for the Western palate. The support of the community, with everyone working together and contributing toward this end, was invaluable in developing a diverse recipe base. I have received many positive comments, especially from people coming from the Asian culinary traditions, on how creative and innovative this collection of recipes is. Over the years, our tastes and metabolisms have changed, new nutritional information has come to light, and new foods have become available, so we felt that revising and adding to this classic book would be a good idea.

¡Buen provecho!
Louise Hagler

Buying and Handling Tofu

Fresh, traditional tofu (that is, tofu prepared with calcium sulfate and magnesium chloride, also known as nigari) can be made or bought in several different forms:

- silken (the softest, most delicate form of tofu)
- medium-soft Japanese-style tofu
- medium-firm Chinese-style tofu
- extra-firm tofu (a very dense, hard-pressed block)

There are many forms available in between these; tofu will vary from soft to firm depending on how it has been processed. Try different brands to discover which ones you like or make your own.

Silken tofu typically comes in an aseptic, shelf-stable carton, sometimes called a tetra-pak, or in a plastic tube. (Traditional silken tofu comes in a water-filled tub.) This type of tofu is not made like traditional tofu, where a coagulant is added to hot soymilk to separate it into curds and whey and the curds are pressed in a mold. For silken tofu, hot soymilk is mixed with a solidifier and then poured directly into the packaging; it thickens and becomes firmer after it is sealed in the container. This type of tofu is softer than traditional tofu and works well in recipes where it is blended or mashed. Silken tofu in aseptic boxes has the advantage of not needing to be refrigerated until it is opened. Because even its firmest form is still relatively soft, it does not hold its shape well when sliced or cubed. Do not try to use this type of tofu in recipes that call for frozen tofu, as it does not respond well to freezing like traditional tofu. For the recipes in this book, traditional tofu will be referred to as "regular tofu" and silken tofu in aseptic packaging will be referred to as "silken tofu."

Once it is opened, tofu will keep for up to one week in the refrigerator. All opened tofu should be kept submerged in cold water in the refrigerator, and the water should be changed daily to keep the tofu fresh and moist. If you make your own tofu or buy it in bulk, handle it this same way, submerged in water in the refrigerator.

Firm traditional tofu may be sliced, cubed, grated, or crumbled. Softer tofu can also be sliced or cubed, but it does not hold its shape well if it is handled a lot. Soft tofu is best when blended, mashed, or crumbled. Remember that different brands of firm tofu may vary in their firmness quite a bit. Try out several brands to see how firm or soft they really are.

If you need a firmer tofu than is available, slice the tofu into equally thick slabs, place the slabs side by side between towels, and set another towel and a heavy breadboard or other similar weight on top of it for 20 to 30 minutes; the towels will absorb the excess water and the tofu will become firmer.

Very fresh tofu has a sweet, delicate scent; this is tofu at its best. Most prepackaged tofu has been pasteurized to help keep it from spoiling and extend its shelf life. Each package of tofu should be stamped with an expiration date. Be sure to check for this when buying tofu; usually the freshest tofu is stocked at the back of the shelf.

Tofu that does not have a sweet, fresh aroma, has turned a shade of pink, or shows signs of slime or mold should be thrown out or composted. If the tofu you buy shows any of these signs or smells very sour, return it to the point of purchase for a replacement, and recommend that the store keep its tofu at a cooler temperature.

Measuring Tofu

There are several different ways to measure tofu when it is not in a premeasured package. Of course, a kitchen scale is very handy for weighing it. If no scale is available, the following methods can be used.

Water Displacement Method

Fill a four-cup measuring cup with three cups of water. Float enough tofu (in a block or cut into cubes) to bring the water level up to four cups. Check the measuring cup at eye level and take care not to press the tofu under the water. This will equal one-half pound of tofu. Drain the water and let the tofu drain on a towel before using.

Dry Measuring Method

To measure mashed or crumbled tofu, pack it into a measuring cup to the one-cup level. This will equal one-half pound of tofu. One-half cup equals one-quarter pound.

Processing or Blending Tofu

The best kitchen appliances for processing or blending tofu with consistently smooth, creamy results are a food processor, a powerful home blender, or a Vita-Mix. When using a standard home blender, it is a good rule to process no more than one-half pound of tofu at a time, unless the tofu is very soft. If the tofu is not very soft, mash or crumble it before processing to put less burden on the blender's motor. Blend tofu as you would any dense food; don't try to process too much at a time, and add liquid as necessary.

Unless it is very soft, tofu processed in a standard home blender will probably need to be gently coaxed from the sides of the blender jar with a rubber spatula to keep it circulating. Be very careful to always keep the spatula well above the blades and never touch the blades with the spatula when the blender is running. If a recipe calls for more than one-half pound of tofu to be processed in a blender along with other ingredients, first break up the tofu in a bowl and mix in the other ingredients. Divide the mixture into smaller batches for blending, using no more than one-half pound of tofu per batch. After processing, mix the batches together well.

If a blender or food processor is not available, an electric mixer will work well with softer tofu.

Freezing Tofu

Freezing traditional tofu transforms it into a unique, chewy, protein-rich food with a meatier texture than regular tofu (see Enchiladas, page 69). When it is frozen, thawed, and gently squeezed dry, tofu resembles a spongy latticework. In this form, tofu readily soaks up marinades and sauces. You can help the tofu absorb marinades or sauces even better by gently pressing down on the pieces with your hand or a spatula and then letting go so the liquid is drawn into the tofu.

To freeze tofu, drain it, wrap it in foil or plastic, and put it in the freezer for at least 24 hours, or until it is frozen into a solid block. When frozen, it will change color from white to a light tan or golden color. If you prefer, cut the tofu into slices or cubes prior to freezing. Tofu will keep in the freezer for up to five months. Let it thaw in the refrigerator, at room temperature, in the microwave, or in boiling water. Freezing tofu adds even more potential to this already versatile food. Do not freeze aseptically packaged silken tofu, as it does not react well to freezing.

Marinating Tofu

Tofu and marinades were meant for each other. Always marinate tofu in a nonreactive container or bowl, such as glass, stainless steel, or enamel with no chips. Marinating slices or cubes of tofu works best in a flat pan (see Korean Barbecue, page 56). The pieces should be carefully turned several times, or use a turkey baster to suck up the marinade and squirt it back over them. For frozen tofu, mix and squeeze the marinade into the pieces. Always marinate tofu in a tightly covered container in the refrigerator to avoid the risk of bacterial growth.

Smoked Tofu

If you have a home smoker, try cutting tofu into blocks or slabs and hot-smoking them. Follow the manufacturer's instructions. Add smoked tofu to salads, use it in sandwiches, or serve it on crackers or in strips as an appetizer. Smoked tofu is also available prepackaged at natural food stores.

Commercially Prepared Tofu

Tofu is widely available with different flavorings, ready to eat. Look for tofu that has been grilled, smoked, marinated, baked, or barbecued, for those days you don't have time to cook. Many natural food stores carry tofu salads and other tofu dishes for takeout in their deli section.

Tofu in various forms and packaging

Rice Paper Rolls with Tofu and Peanut Dipping Sauce

appet

Appetizers, Dips, and Spreads

Tofu can be transformed into a variety of mouthwatering appetizers, from finger foods to dips and spreads. In addition to Veggie Sushi (page 8) and Rice Paper Rolls (page 10), consider serving bite-size Cucumber Finger Sandwiches (page 39), Lettuce Rolls (page 41), Mediterranean Spring Rolls (page 114), Spring Rolls (page 112), Tofu Knishes (page 117), Tofu Turnovers (page 116), Taquitos (page 115), Wontons (page 111), or Chewy Tofu Nuggets (page 58). Along with the dips and spreads in this chapter, tofu salads such as Salad sans Poulet (page 35), Savory Tofu Salad (page 38), Golden Tofu Salad (page 37), Sesame Tofu Salad (page 40), and Cottage Tofu Salad (page 37) can be served on crackers or with chips and raw vegetables.

Veggie Sushi

MAKES 6 TO 8 SERVINGS

In Japan, sushi is equivalent in popularity to the sandwich in America; it can be found everywhere.

Making sushi is an art form that chefs specialize in and study for many years. Sushi is widely available now in the West, even in supermarkets, but it is easy and fun to make at home. It makes great party food and can be served as a snack, a meal, or an appetizer made with a variety of fillings. It travels well and is usually served at room temperature.

All of the ingredients for sushi can be prepared in advance and refrigerated, ready to be put together on a moment's notice. There is a short-grain Japanese-style rice used especially for sushi. You can substitute brown rice if you like, but it doesn't quite stick together as well as sushi rice and changes the overall flavor. Either rice can be cooked in a rice cooker or on the stove.

Sushi nori, or dried laver as it is sometimes called, is available toasted or plain. You can toast it at home, if you prefer. There are many different grades of sushi nori, usually distinguishable by price; that is, the higher the price, the higher the grade. Sushi nori usually comes in packages of ten 8 x 7-inch sheets.

Wasabi is Japanese horseradish, which comes powdered (and must be mixed with water before using) or already prepared in a tube. A little goes a long way with wasabi, as it tends to be hot enough to clear out the sinuses.

Pickled ginger is a condiment served with sushi. It can be bought already prepared, ready to serve.

FOR THE SUSHI RICE

Wash and drain 3 to 4 times with cold water until the water is almost clear:

> 3 cups Japanese-style short-grain sushi rice

Put the rice in a heavy pot along with:

> 3¾ cups cold water

Cover the pot and bring to a boil over high heat. When it reaches a rapid boil, turn the heat down to low without lifting the lid and simmer for 25 minutes. Remove from the heat and let stand covered another 10 minutes. (If you are using a rice cooker, reduce the water to 3 cups.)

While the rice is standing, mix in a small bowl and stir until the sweetener is dissolved:

> ½ cup rice vinegar
>
> 6 tablespoons sweetener of your choice
>
> 2 teaspoons salt

Fluff the rice with a fork and transfer it to a 9 x 13-inch pan. Have ready a small electric fan directed at the pan, a person available to hold an electric hair dryer on the cold setting pointed at the pan, or someone available to manually fan the rice. While the rice is being fanned, carefully stir and fold in the vinegar mixture with a bamboo paddle. Be careful not to mash the rice; the grains should remain whole and separate. The rice will be somewhat sticky; this is the desired result.

FOR THE TOFU

Mix together in a small bowl or measuring cup:

> 2 tablespoons peeled and grated fresh ginger
>
> 2 tablespoons mirin
>
> 2 cloves garlic, pressed
>
> 1 tablespoon soy sauce

Cut into long strips about ¼ inch square:

> ¾ pound firm or extra-firm regular tofu

Arrange the tofu strips in a single layer in a flat-bottomed glass or stainless steel pan and pour the ginger mixture over them. Let the tofu marinate in the refrigerator for at least 30 minutes.

Brown the marinated tofu in a small amount of olive oil in a nonstick pan or griddle.

FOR THE VEGETABLES

Cut into long, ¼-inch-wide strips:

> 1 to 2 cucumbers, peeled and seeded
>
> 1 to 2 ripe avocados
>
> 1 red bell pepper

Squeeze and sprinkle over the vegetables:

> 3 to 4 tablespoons freshly squeezed lemon juice

Rinse, drain, and set aside:

> 4 ounces fresh sprouts (such as alfalfa, sunflower, or mung bean)

FOR THE WASABI

Mix together with a fork until a ball is formed:

> 4 tablespoons wasabi powder
>
> ¼ cup water

This should be enough for 6 to 8 people who like wasabi.

PUTTING IT ALL TOGETHER

Have ready:

> 10 sheets toasted sushi nori

Making the sushi rolls is similar to rolling a giant cigar or small jellyroll. Lay a bamboo rolling mat (called a *sudare*) flat in front of you with the slats running horizontally. The mat will help you get the rolling started evenly. Lay a sheet of toasted sushi nori on the mat, centered near the end closest to you. If you want to roll the sushi with the rice on the outside of the roll (rather than the nori), cover the mat with plastic wrap.

Keep a bowl of cold water nearby to keep your hands moist while working with the rice. Cover the bottom three-quarters of the nori sheet with 1 cup of the rice that has been divided into 2 equal mounds. Dip your hands or fingers in the bowl of water as necessary while pushing the rice into place evenly across the nori, using both your fingers and the heels of your palms.

When the rice is evenly in place, spread it over the nori within 1 to 2 inches from the top, keeping it about ⅛ to ¼ inch thick. Lay single strips of the tofu, bell pepper, cucumber, and avocado, and about ½ ounce of sprouts in a horizontal line in the center of the rice, covering it from side to side.

Starting with the end of the mat closest to you, lift the rice-covered nori up and over the vegetables while holding the vegetables in place. Tuck the edge of the nori under the vegetables, roll the mat slightly back away from the nori (so the mat doesn't get rolled into the sushi), and simultaneously roll the sushi into a cylinder, free from the mat. Use a little pressure while working to form a tight roll, and press any loose ingredients back into the ends of the roll when you are done. It is okay if some of the filling protrudes from the ends, as it will make an interesting presentation when those pieces are set upright. Place the roll on a cutting board and cut it into 8 equal rounds with a wet knife. Wipe the knife and remoisten it as necessary. Arrange the rounds, cut side down, on a platter, and sprinkle the top of each piece with sesame seeds. Serve with small dishes of soy sauce, pickled ginger, and the wasabi paste.

Rice Paper Rolls WITH TOFU AND PEANUT DIPPING SAUCE

These light, fresh rolls, inspired by Vietnamese and Thai cuisine, are mostly raw, with tofu added for protein. Rice paper sheets are available in most Asian markets. These rolls make a great hands-on treat for party fare. They take a little practice to make, but if the first try doesn't work out perfectly, they will still be edible and delicious. Rice Paper Rolls are pictured on page 6.

Have ready:

> 1 pound firm regular tofu, cut into 3 x ¼-inch sticks
>
> 20 round rice paper sheets (8 or 9 inches in diameter)

FOR THE FILLING

Any combination of these will work; use whatever appeals to you:

> Avocado, thinly sliced
>
> Bibb or Boston lettuce
>
> Carrot, finely shredded
>
> English cucumber, seeded and cut into matchsticks
>
> Fresh cilantro leaves
>
> Fresh mint leaves
>
> Fresh shiitake mushroom caps, thinly sliced and browned in olive oil
>
> Green onions, finely chopped
>
> Jicama or daikon radish, cut into matchsticks or shredded
>
> Mung bean threads or rice sticks, soaked in hot water for about 30 minutes and drained
>
> Red bell pepper, thinly sliced
>
> Sprouts (mung bean, daikon radish, or alfalfa)
>
> Small fresh basil leaves

PUTTING IT ALL TOGETHER

Fill a flat-bottomed 10-inch bowl or roasting pan with warm to hot water. Add one rice paper sheet at a time to soften. This will take from a few to several seconds, depending on the brand. The sheet may still be slightly stiff in a few spots—don't let it get too soft. Remove the sheet from the water and place it on a plate, cutting board, or counter covered with a towel. If you want to soften several rice paper sheets at a time, let them drain on a kitchen towel.

Place one piece of lettuce on top of the softened rice paper. Arrange your choice of fillings in line across the lower third of each lettuce piece, leaving a 1-inch border all the way around. Don't add too much filling or the roll will be too fat. Fold the bottom of each rice paper over the lettuce and filling, then fold in the ends and roll into a tight cylinder. The rice paper should stick together without tearing. Place the rolls, seam side down, on a platter.

The rolls are best made fresh, right before serving, but they can be made up to 6 hours in advance and covered with damp paper towels and plastic wrap. Just before serving, cut each roll diagonally into halves or thirds. Arrange them on a platter and serve with Peanut Dipping Sauce (recipe follows).

PEANUT DIPPING SAUCE

Makes 1 cup

This sauce can be made a day in advance and refrigerated, but bring it to room temperature at least 30 minutes before serving to let the flavors meld.

Chop in a food processor:

> 1 piece (½-inch cube) peeled fresh ginger
>
> 1 clove garlic

Add and process until smooth:

> ¼ cup soy sauce
>
> ¼ cup freshly squeezed lime juice
>
> ¼ cup sweetener of your choice
>
> ¼ cup unsalted natural peanut butter
>
> ¼ cup minced fresh Thai basil (optional)
>
> ⅛ to ¼ teaspoon crushed red pepper flakes or cayenne

Dips and Spreads

For dips, medium-soft to firm regular tofu, Japanese-style tofu, or aseptically packaged silken tofu are best. Dips can be prepared with a food processor, blender, or electric mixer (see Processing or Blending Tofu, page 4). Use only very fresh tofu for making dips. For lower-calorie dips and spreads, leave out the optional oil. For an extra boost of omega-3 and omega-6 essential fatty acids, use flaxseed oil, hempseed oil, or chia seed oil in recipes that don't require cooking. Most dips are best if you make them in advance and let the flavors fully develop for several hours in the refrigerator.

Roasted Red Pepper Dip, page 14, and Cilantro-Jalapeño Dip, page 15

Garlic-Cucumber Dip

This is a tofu-based version of Greek tzatziki, which is traditionally made with yogurt.

Chop in a food processor or blender or by hand and transfer to a small bowl:

  1 small cucumber, peeled and seeded
  1 tablespoon minced fresh dill, or 1 teaspoon dried
  1 clove garlic

Process in a food processor or blender until smooth and creamy:

  ½ pound firm regular tofu, mashed or crumbled

  1 tablespoon olive oil (optional)
  1 tablespoon white wine vinegar
  1 teaspoon sweetener of your choice
  ½ teaspoon salt

Stir the tofu mixture into the cucumber. Chill thoroughly before serving.

Wasabi-Ginger Dip or Spread

Here is a dip that packs a punch. It's great with raw veggies, chips, or crackers.

Chop in a food processor or blender:

  1 piece (½-inch cube) peeled fresh ginger
  1 clove garlic

Add and process until smooth and creamy:

  ½ pound firm regular tofu, mashed or crumbled

  1 tablespoon wasabi powder
  1 tablespoon soy sauce

Note: Add the wasabi powder to taste; it can be overpowering for some people.

Walnut-Olive Dip

Process in a food processor or blender until smooth and creamy:

  ½ pound firm regular tofu, mashed or crumbled
  3 tablespoons freshly squeezed lemon juice
  1 tablespoon olive oil (optional)

  2 teaspoons sweetener of your choice
  ½ teaspoon salt

Fold in:

  2 tablespoons finely chopped walnuts
  4 teaspoons chopped black olives

Dried Onion Soup Dip

This is the classic California dip made with tofu instead of sour cream.

Process in a food processor or blender until smooth and creamy:

> 1 pound soft regular tofu, mashed or crumbled
>
> 2 tablespoons olive oil (optional)
>
> 2 tablespoons freshly squeezed lemon juice
>
> 1 tablespoon sweetener of your choice

Stir or process in:

> 1 package (1.25 ounces) dried onion soup mix

If time permits, refrigerate for 4 to 12 hours to let the flavors blend.

VARIATION

If you'd rather not use a packaged mix to flavor this dip, replace it with:

> ⅓ cup dried minced onions
>
> 1 tablespoon vegetable bouillon powder
>
> 1 teaspoon garlic powder

Chive Dip

Process in a food processor or blender until smooth and creamy:

> 1 pound soft regular tofu, mashed or crumbled
>
> 2 tablespoons olive oil (optional)
>
> 1 tablespoon apple cider vinegar or white wine vinegar

> 1 tablespoon soy sauce
>
> ½ teaspoon garlic powder
>
> ¼ teaspoon freshly ground black pepper

Fold in:

> ½ cup chopped fresh chives

Dill Dip

Process in a food processor or blender until smooth and creamy:

> ¾ cup soft regular tofu, mashed or crumbled
>
> 2½ tablespoons wine vinegar
>
> 1 tablespoon olive oil (optional)

> 1 tablespoon minced onion
>
> 1 tablespoon minced fresh dill, or 1 teaspoon dried
>
> 1½ teaspoons sweetener of your choice
>
> 1 teaspoon salt
>
> ⅛ teaspoon freshly ground black pepper

Roasted Red Pepper Dip

This is great as a sandwich filling, spread for crackers, or a dip. Roasted red bell peppers and pimientos can be purchased canned or bottled, already peeled and chopped. Alternatively, they can be roasted and prepared at home.

To roast the pepper at home, char over a gas flame on the stovetop or under a broiler:

> 1 medium-size red bell pepper or fresh pimiento

Place the charred pepper in a closed plastic or paper bag for 15 to 20 minutes. Remove it from the bag and peel off all of the charred skin using your fingers. Rinse the pepper under running water, if needed, and drain. Remove and discard the seeds and membranes and chop the flesh. Set aside ½ cup of the chopped pepper and store the remainder in the refrigerator to use in another recipe.

Process in a food processor or blender until smooth and creamy:

> ¼ pound soft regular tofu, mashed or crumbled (½ cup)
> 2 tablespoons olive oil (optional)
> 2 tablespoons apple cider vinegar
> 1 tablespoon sweetener of your choice
> 1 teaspoon salt
> ⅛ teaspoon freshly ground black pepper
> Dash of garlic powder

Fold in:

> ¾ pound firm regular tofu, crumbled
> ½ cup chopped roasted red peppers or pimientos
> 3 tablespoons sweet pickle relish (optional)

Refrigerate for 8 to 12 hours to let the flavors blend.

Garlic Dip

Chop in a food processor or blender:

> 4 cloves garlic

Add and process until smooth and creamy:

> ½ pound soft regular tofu, mashed or crumbled
> 2 tablespoons olive oil (optional)
> 2 tablespoons freshly squeezed lemon juice
> 1 tablespoon sweetener of your choice
> ½ teaspoon salt

Almond Dip

Process in a food processor or blender until smooth and creamy:

> ½ pound soft regular tofu, mashed or crumbled
> 3 tablespoons freshly squeezed lemon juice
> 1 tablespoon olive oil (optional)
> 2 teaspoons sweetener of your choice
> ½ teaspoon salt

Fold in:

> ¼ cup roasted slivered almonds

Jalapeño Dip

This dip is for folks who like it hot!

Process in a food processor or blender until smooth and creamy:

  ¾ pound soft regular tofu, mashed or crumbled
  ½ small onion, chopped
  2 tablespoons olive oil (optional)
  1 to 2 pickled jalapeño chiles

2 tablespoons chopped fresh cilantro or parsley
½ teaspoon salt

Chill for at least 2 hours before serving.

Note: This dip is spicy hot (*picante*) by American standards, and gets even hotter after it has been chilled.

Cilantro-Jalapeño Dip

Serve this light green dip with red, blue, or yellow corn chips or raw vegetables. Cilantro-Jalapeño Dip is pictured on page 11.

Chop in a food processor or blender:

  1 cup fresh cilantro leaves, loosely packed
  1 clove garlic
  1 small jalapeño chile

Add and process until smooth and creamy:

  ½ pound soft regular tofu, mashed or crumbled
  1 tablespoon olive oil (optional)

1 tablespoon freshly squeezed lime or lemon juice
½ teaspoon salt

Note: Add the jalapeño with care, as chiles vary in "heat." You might want to start with half the chile, sample the dip, and add more to taste. For a less spicy dip, remove the seeds and membranes from the chile.

Miso-Ginger Dip

Chop in a food processor or blender:

  1 piece (1½-inch cube) peeled fresh ginger
  1 piece (1-inch cube) onion
  1 clove garlic

Add and process until smooth and creamy:

  ½ pound firm regular tofu, mashed or crumbled

2 tablespoons mellow white miso
1½ tablespoons freshly squeezed lemon juice

Note: Fresh ginger can vary in intensity from piece to piece. Add it to taste.

Guacamole Dip

Mash:

   2 ripe avocados

Stir in:

   ¾ cup chopped fresh tomato

   ½ cup Tofu Salad Dressing (page 50)

   ½ cup green taco sauce

¼ cup minced onion, or 2 teaspoons onion powder

1 to 3 cloves garlic, pressed, or 1 teaspoon garlic powder

½ teaspoon salt

Serve immediately.

Creamy Chipotle Dip

Chipotles en adobo are red jalapeño chiles that have been smoked and then cooked in a tomato sauce; they are available in cans at most supermarkets. These are spicy-hot chiles, so check them for your picante tolerance.

Process in a food processor or blender until smooth and creamy:

   ½ pound firm regular tofu, mashed or crumbled

1 to 2 chipotles en adobo

2 tablespoons freshly squeezed lime juice

½ to 1 teaspoon salt

Curry Paste Dip

This is excellent with raw vegetables. Commercial curry pastes vary in spiciness, so taste yours before adding the full amount.

Process in a food processor or blender until smooth and creamy:

   ½ pound soft regular tofu, mashed or crumbled

   3 tablespoons curry paste

   2 tablespoons freshly squeezed lemon juice

Fold in:

   1 cup peeled, seeded, and chopped cucumber

Caper Spread

Used in Mediterranean cuisine, a caper is a pickled or salted flower bud from a special shrub cultivated in Europe. Capers are used as condiments in sauces and dressings.

Process in a food processor or blender until smooth and creamy:

> ½ pound soft regular tofu, mashed or crumbled
>
> 2 tablespoons caper brine
>
> 1 tablespoon olive oil (optional)
>
> 1 teaspoon Dijon mustard
>
> ½ teaspoon salt

Pour into a bowl rubbed with:

> 1 clove garlic, cut in half

Fold in:

> 1 tablespoon minced onion
>
> 1 tablespoon capers (if the capers are large, cut them in half)

Parsley-Onion Dip

Process in a food processor or blender until smooth and creamy:

> 1 pound firm regular tofu, mashed or crumbled
>
> ½ cup fresh parsley leaves
>
> 1 small red onion, chopped (about ⅓ cup), or 2 teaspoons onion powder
>
> 2 tablespoons olive oil (optional)
>
> 2 tablespoons freshly squeezed lemon juice
>
> 1 teaspoon salt

Green Onion Dip

Try this light green dip in the spring with fresh green onions.

Chop in a food processor or blender:

> ½ cup chopped green onions
>
> ½ cup fresh parsley leaves, loosely packed

Add and process until smooth and creamy:

> ½ pound soft regular tofu, mashed or crumbled
>
> 1 tablespoon freshly squeezed lemon juice
>
> 1 tablespoon olive oil (optional)
>
> ¼ teaspoon salt

Zucchini Bisque

soup

Soups

A soup is only as tasty as its base. Powdered vegetable bouillon, vegetable bouillon cubes, vegetable broth in aseptic cartons, and miso offer quick and tasty solutions for soup stock. Whether a soup is creamy or chunky, tofu will add protein and personality. Try it in a variety of forms, such as chewy frozen tofu, creamy blended tofu, or soft cubes. If you use blended tofu for creating creamy soups, don't let the soup boil after you have added it, as it could curdle. Hot soups make great comfort food in cold weather, and cold soups are refreshing and cooling in hot weather. With so much versatility, soup is ideal for year-round fare.

Zucchini Bisque

Blended tofu thickens this soup and makes it creamy. Zucchini Bisque is pictured on page 18.

Heat in a 3-quart soup pot over medium heat:

> 2 tablespoons olive oil

Cook and stir in the heated oil over medium heat until the onion is soft:

> 1½ pounds zucchini, sliced
>
> 1 medium-size onion, chopped

Stir in:

> 2½ cups vegetable broth or water
>
> ½ teaspoon freshly grated nutmeg
>
> ⅛ teaspoon freshly ground black pepper

Cover and simmer for 20 minutes. Remove from the heat and let cool for 5 minutes.

Process in a blender until smooth and creamy:

> ½ pound soft regular tofu, mashed or crumbled
>
> 1 tablespoon olive oil (optional)

Stir the tofu mixture into the soup. Heat but do not boil. Season with salt to taste.

Cucumber Gazpacho

This is a cool, refreshing way to make use of the cucumber bounty in summer. Kirby cucumbers are my favorite kind to use in this soup, because they are more substantial in flavor and less watery than other types. To ensure a smooth soup, process it in at least two batches.

FOR THE SOUP

Process in a food processor or blender until smooth and creamy:

> 2½ pounds cucumbers, peeled, seeded, and coarsely chopped (about 5½ cups)
>
> 2 cups plain, unsweetened soy yogurt
>
> ¼ cup freshly squeezed lime juice
>
> 3 tablespoons olive oil
>
> 3 tablespoons sweet white miso, or 1½ teaspoons salt
>
> 1 clove garlic
>
> ¼ teaspoon freshly ground black pepper

Pour into a container and refrigerate until thoroughly chilled.

FOR THE TOPPINGS

Have ready:

> 1 tomato, sliced
>
> ½ pound firm regular tofu, cut into very small cubes
>
> Fresh basil or cilantro, chopped

Spoon the chilled soup into serving bowls and float a slice of tomato on the top of each one. Top with 2 tablespoons of the tofu cubes and a good sprinkling of the basil or cilantro.

Quick Vegetable Miso Soup with Tofu

No chopping is required for this soup—use prechopped frozen vegetables, canned tomatoes, and prepared pesto. Add the miso last, dissolved in some of the soup broth. Don't let the soup boil after the miso has been added or the soup may curdle and the miso's valuable enzymes will be destroyed.

Heat in a 3-quart soup pot over medium heat:

> 2 tablespoons olive oil

Add and stir over medium heat until thawed:

> ½ pound frozen mixed colored bell peppers and onions
>
> ½ pound frozen mixed vegetables

Stir in:

> 1 can (14.5 ounces) fire-roasted tomatoes
>
> 2 cans (14.5 ounces each) water

Bring to a boil and add:

> ½ pound firm regular tofu, cut into small cubes
>
> 2 tablespoons prepared dairy-free basil pesto

Remove from the heat, transfer 1 cup of the soup broth to a bowl, and stir in:

> 2 to 3 tablespoons chickpea miso or other miso of your choice.

Mix until the miso is dissolved in the broth, and then stir it into the soup. Serve immediately.

Mushroom-Tofu Noodle Soup

Chewy frozen tofu adds texture and protein to this warming comfort food.

Have ready:

> 1 pound firm regular tofu, frozen, thawed, squeezed dry, and finely chopped

Heat in a 4-quart soup pot over medium heat:

> 2 tablespoons olive oil

Cook and stir in the heated oil until the vegetables are crisp-tender:

> 1 medium-size onion, chopped
>
> 6 ounces mushrooms, sliced
>
> 1 cup thinly sliced carrots
>
> 1 cup chopped celery
>
> ¾ cup chopped green bell pepper
>
> 2 cloves garlic, minced

When the vegetables are almost done, stir in the prepared tofu. Then add:

> 8 cups water
>
> 6 cubes vegetable bouillon, or 2 tablespoons vegetable bouillon powder

Bring the soup to a boil and add:

> 6 to 8 ounces semolina or whole wheat flat noodles

Boil for about 10 minutes, or until the noodles are just tender. Serve immediately.

Minestrone

Here is the vegan version of this Italian classic.

Have ready:

>   1 pound firm regular tofu, frozen, thawed, squeezed dry, and cut into ¾-inch cubes

Preheat the oven to 375 degrees F, and oil an 11 x 17-inch baking sheet with olive oil. Mix together in a small bowl or measuring cup:

>   3 tablespoons soy sauce
>   1 clove garlic, pressed, or ½ teaspoon garlic powder

Squeeze this mixture into the tofu cubes (see Freezing Tofu, page 4). Arrange the tofu on the prepared baking sheet and bake for 10 minutes. Turn the cubes over and bake for 5 minutes longer. Remove from the oven and set aside.

Heat in a 4-quart soup pot over medium heat:

>   2 tablespoons olive oil

Cook and stir in the heated oil over medium heat until crisp-tender:

>   1 medium-size onion, chopped
>   2 carrots, sliced
>   1 medium-size zucchini, sliced

Stir in:

>   1 can (28 ounces) diced or chopped tomatoes, with juice
>   4 cups water
>   2 cups tomato juice
>   2 tablespoons minced fresh basil, or 2 teaspoons dried
>   1 tablespoon minced fresh oregano, or 1 teaspoon dried
>   1 clove garlic, pressed, or ½ teaspoon garlic powder
>   ½ teaspoon salt
>   ¼ teaspoon freshly ground black pepper

Bring to a boil and add:

>   3 ounces semolina or whole wheat noodles or broken spaghetti

Simmer for 5 minutes. Then stir in the browned tofu cubes and:

>   1 can (15 ounces) kidney beans, rinsed and drained

Simmer until the beans and tofu are heated through and the pasta is tender.

Minstrone Soup with a sandwich of Basic Fried Tofu, page 64

Curried Tofu-Apple Soup

This is a mild curried soup, slightly sweetened with apples.

Have ready:

> 1½ pounds firm regular tofu, frozen, thawed, squeezed dry, and cut or torn into bite-size pieces

Wash, peel, and dice:

> 4 to 5 medium-size apples

Bring to a boil in a 4-quart soup pot:

> 2 quarts vegetable broth or water

Add the apples and boil for 2 minutes. Strain and return the cooking liquid to the soup pot. Set the cooking liquid and apples aside separately.

Heat in a large skillet or sauté pan over low heat:

> ¼ cup canola oil

Cook and stir in the heated oil over low heat until almost transparent:

> ½ cup chopped onion

Add the tofu pieces and lightly brown them. While the onions and tofu are cooking, sprinkle them with:

> ⅓ cup unbleached flour
>
> 2 tablespoons curry powder
>
> 2 teaspoons salt

Cook and stir briefly. Then stir in the cooked apples and 2 cups of the reserved cooking liquid.

Stir constantly over medium heat, taking care to avoid any lumps. Pour the mixture into the soup pot with the remaining reserved cooking liquid. Bring to a boil over medium heat, stir, cover, and simmer for 10 to 15 minutes.

Tofu Chowder

Tofu is a perfect fit with chowder, and you can leave the clams snug in their beach home.

Heat in a 3-quart soup pot over low heat:

> 2 tablespoons olive oil

Cook and stir in the heated oil over low heat until the vegetables are crisp-tender:

> 1 medium-size onion, chopped
>
> 3 stalks celery, chopped
>
> 2 carrots, chopped

Stir in:

> 2 large potatoes, peeled and cubed (about 2 cups)

> 2 cups water
>
> 2 cups unsweetened soymilk
>
> ½ pound firm regular tofu, crumbled
>
> 2 teaspoons salt
>
> ½ teaspoon freshly ground black pepper
>
> ½ teaspoon celery seeds

Bring to a boil, lower the heat, and simmer until the potatoes are soft.

Watercress Soup

This delicately flavored soup can be made with several delicious variations. Watercress Soup with Wontons is pictured on the opposite page.

Dissolve together in a 3-quart soup pot:

> 2 quarts boiling water
>
> 4 cubes vegetable bouillon

Stir in:

> ½ pound firm regular tofu, cut into 1½ x ¼ x ¼-inch pieces
>
> 1 small onion, diced or sliced into rounds

Simmer for 10 minutes. Then stir in:

> 1 bunch watercress, coarsely chopped

Cook for 3 minutes longer. Serve immediately.

VARIATIONS

Bok Choy Soup: Omit the watercress. Chop ½ pound bok choy diagonally every ½ inch; separate the stem and leaf pieces. Add the stem pieces to the soup 4 to 5 minutes before serving; add the leaf pieces 3 minutes before serving.

Watercress Soup with Wontons or Noodles: Add about 25 Wontons (page 111) during the last 5 minutes of cooking, or add 4 ounces semolina or whole wheat flat noodles along with the onion and tofu.

Tomato Soup WITH CHICKPEAS AND CUMIN

Try this hearty soup on a cold winter day.

Have ready:

> ½ pound firm regular tofu, frozen, thawed, squeezed dry, and cut into ¼-inch cubes

Heat in a 3-quart soup pot over medium heat:

> 2 tablespoons olive oil

Cook and stir in the heated oil until tender:

> 1 small zucchini, sliced (about 1½ cups)
>
> 1 cup sliced spring onions (white and green parts)
>
> ½ cup chopped green bell pepper
>
> 1 cup sliced carrots
>
> ½ cup sliced celery
>
> 1 clove garlic, minced or pressed

In a small dry pan, toast over medium heat and then grind:

> 1 tablespoon cumin seeds

> ¼ teaspoon cracked red pepper

Stir the ground spices into the cooking vegetables. Then stir in:

> 4 cups water or vegetable broth
>
> 1 can (15 ounces) fire-roasted chopped tomatoes, with juice
>
> 1 can (15 ounces) chickpeas, rinsed and drained
>
> 1 teaspoon salt

Stir in the prepared tofu, bring to a boil, and then stir in:

> ½ cup chopped fresh cilantro

Remove from the heat and serve.

Tomato-Rice Soup with Tofu

This soup is comfort food. It welcomes tofu and leftover cooked rice.

Heat in a 2-quart sauce pan over low heat:

  1 tablespoon olive oil

Cook and stir in the heated oil over low heat until soft:

  ⅔ cup chopped green bell pepper
  ⅔ cup chopped onion
  1 clove garlic, minced

Process in a blender or food processor until smooth:

  1 can (16 ounces) plum tomatoes with juice, or 1 pound fresh tomatoes, skins removed
  2 cups water

Stir the blended tomatoes into the soup pot along with:

  1 cup cooked brown rice
  ¼ pound firm regular tofu, cut into small cubes
  1 tablespoon chopped fresh parsley, or 1 teaspoon dried
  1 tablespoon chopped fresh basil, or 1 teaspoon dried
  ½ teaspoon salt
  ¼ teaspoon freshly ground black pepper
  ¼ teaspoon ground allspice

Stir well and simmer until heated through.

Lentil Soup

Tofu adds more protein and texture to this hearty soup.

Bring to a boil in a 3-quart soup pot:

  1 quart boiling water
  1 cup dried lentils, washed and drained

Lower the heat and let simmer while you prepare the vegetables.

Heat in a medium-size skillet or sauté pan over low heat:

  2 tablespoons olive oil

Cook and stir over low heat until crisp-tender:

  1 medium-size onion, chopped
  1 medium-size carrot, sliced
  1 stalk celery, sliced
  1 clove garlic, minced

Stir the cooked vegetables into the soup pot along with:

  1 cup peeled, chopped tomatoes, or 1 can (3 ounces) tomato paste
  1 teaspoon salt

Simmer until the lentils are soft. Then stir in:

  ½ pound firm regular tofu, cut into small cubes
  1 tablespoon minced fresh basil, or 1 teaspoon dried
  1½ teaspoons wine vinegar
  ⅛ teaspoon freshly ground black pepper

Simmer until heated through.

Miso Soup

Miso is a flavorful, salty, cultured, and fermented bean paste from which soy sauce evolved. It can be found in natural food stores or Asian markets. Unpasteurized miso contains beneficial enzymes that are lost when miso is boiled, so always remove soup from the heat before stirring it in. Another benefit of miso is that it binds with toxins in the body and carries them out.

Heat in a 3-quart soup pot over medium heat:

    2 tablespoons olive oil

Cook and stir in the heated oil over medium heat until limp but not brown:

    1 small head cabbage, shredded
    3 to 4 small onions, diced
    4 to 6 carrots, sliced
    3 stalks celery, sliced

Stir in:

    2 quarts hot water

    1 pound firm regular tofu, cut into ½-inch cubes
    1 teaspoon salt

Simmer until the vegetables are tender and the tofu is heated through. Dissolve in 1 cup of the soup broth:

    ¼ cup red miso, or 6 tablespoons white miso

Remove the soup from the heat and stir in the miso mixture along with:

    ¼ teaspoon freshly ground black pepper

Miso Soup with Tofu and Wakame

Enjoy the benefits of miso, tofu, and wakame in this classic miso soup. Mineral-rich wakame is a sea vegetable with a mild flavor and a delicate leaf. It contains an abundance of calcium and B vitamins, as well as vitamin C. Serve this soup for breakfast with brown rice or with any meal.

Heat to boiling in a 3-quart soup pot:

    6 cups water

Stir in and simmer:

    1 cup carrots, cut into matchsticks
    ½ pound firm or extra-firm tofu, cut into ½ x ¼ x ¹⁄₁₆-inch pieces

When the carrots are crisp-tender (1 to 2 minutes), stir in:

    ⅓ cup dried wakame

Simmer for 1 minute, then remove from the heat. Stir together until the miso is dissolved:

    ½ cup water
    ¼ cup red miso, or 6 tablespoons mellow white miso

Stir the miso mixture into the soup. Ladle the soup into individual bowls and top each serving with a sprinkling of:

    Green onions, chopped
    Sesame seeds

Hot-and-Sour Soup

This is a classic Chinese soup.

Bring to a boil in a 3-quart soup pot:

> 4 cups water

Stir in and simmer for 3 minutes:

> 2 cups thinly sliced cabbage
>
> ½ pound firm or extra-firm regular tofu, cut into matchsticks
>
> 1 tablespoon soy sauce
>
> 2 cubes vegetable bouillon
>
> ¾ teaspoon salt

Stir in:

> 2 tablespoons white wine vinegar
>
> ¼ teaspoon cayenne

Bring the soup back to a boil. Stir together in a small bowl or measuring cup:

> 3 tablespoons cold water
>
> 2 tablespoons cornstarch

Stir the cornstarch mixture into the soup and simmer for a few minutes until it is slightly thickened.

Garnish each serving with:

> Green onions, chopped
>
> 2 teaspoons toasted sesame oil (optional)

Spring Soup

MAKES 6 CUPS

This soup matches tofu with your favorite spring vegetables.

Have ready:

> ½ pound firm regular tofu, frozen, thawed, squeezed dry, and cut into bite-size pieces

Heat in a 2-quart saucepan or soup pot over medium heat:

> 2 tablespoons olive oil

Cook and stir in the heated oil over medium heat until crisp-tender:

> 1 cup chopped green onions
>
> 1 carrot, thinly sliced on the diagonal
>
> 1 stalk celery, thinly sliced on the diagonal
>
> ¼ cup chopped fresh parsley
>
> 2 cloves garlic, minced

Stir in:

> 4 cups boiling water

Bring to a boil and stir in the tofu along with:

> 1 cup fresh or frozen green peas
>
> 1 cup chopped fresh spinach or watercress
>
> 1 bay leaf

Simmer until the peas are tender. Remove the bay leaf before serving.

Mexican Corn Soup

This is a thick and hearty savory soup. Remove the seeds from the chile for a milder soup.

Have ready:

> ½ pound firm regular tofu, frozen, thawed, squeezed dry, and cut into small pieces

Heat in a 4-quart soup pot over low heat:

> 2 tablespoons olive oil

Cook and stir in the heated oil over low heat until soft:

> 1 cup chopped onion
> ¾ cup chopped green bell pepper
> 3 cloves garlic, minced

Stir into the pot:

> 4 cups water
> 1 can (15 ounces) chopped or diced tomatoes, with juice

1 can (30 ounces) hominy, drained
1 cup fresh or frozen green peas
1 tablespoon minced fresh oregano, or 1 teaspoon dried
½ medium-size jalapeño chile, thinly sliced
1 teaspoon ground cumin

Raise the heat to medium-high and stir in the tofu and:

> ¼ cup minced fresh cilantro

Bring to a boil and simmer until heated through. Ladle into soup bowls and garnish each serving with:

> Avocado slices
> Corn tortillas, cut into thin strips

Greek Salad

sala

Salads

Versatile tofu can be the main event in a salad, or blended into a creamy dressing to top a salad, or both! Because tofu is rich in protein, tofu-based salads tend to work best as a main course; but in smaller portions, they can also serve well as a side dish. Adapted from many different cultural cuisines, these salads offer choices that are sure to please any palate. Whether they include chewy and flavorful frozen tofu or soft, delicate, traditional tofu, salads welcome many forms of this versatile, high-protein food. Try adding smoked tofu to tossed green salads for a special treat.

Greek Salad

GREEK SALA

Marinated tofu replaces feta cheese in this classic salad for a crowd. Greek Salad is pictured on page 30.

FOR THE TOFU AND DRESSING

To make the dressing, mix together in a small bowl or measuring cup:

> ¼ cup olive oil
>
> 2 tablespoons wine vinegar
>
> 1½ tablespoons sweet white miso, or 1 teaspoon salt
>
> 1 tablespoon minced fresh basil, or 1 teaspoon dried
>
> 1½ teaspoons minced fresh oregano, or ½ teaspoon dried
>
> ½ teaspoon freshly ground black pepper

Arrange in a 7 x 11-inch glass or stainless steel pan:

> 1 pound firm or extra-firm regular tofu, cut into ¾-inch cubes

Pour the dressing over the tofu, stir gently, cover, and marinate in the refrigerator for at least 1 hour, gently stirring occasionally.

FOR THE SALAD

Toss together in a large bowl:

> 3 ripe tomatoes, cut into wedges
>
> 3 cucumbers, thinly sliced
>
> ½ large red onion, chopped
>
> ½ cup Greek or black olives

Stir in the tofu and dressing. Serve on mesclun or leaf lettuce.

Almond Salad

ALMOND SALA

Roasted almonds add crunch and flavor to this creamy salad.

Combine in a large bowl:

> 1½ pounds firm or extra-firm regular tofu, cut into ½-inch cubes
>
> 3 tablespoons freshly squeezed lemon juice
>
> ½ teaspoon celery salt

Mix in:

> 1½ cups diced celery
>
> ¾ cup roasted slivered almonds
>
> ⅓ cup minced green onions
>
> ½ teaspoon salt

Stir in:

> 1½ cups Tofu Sour Creamy Dressing (page 50)

Chill thoroughly before serving. Serve on a bed of mesclun or leaf lettuce, or stuff the salad into a hollowed-out tomato or red bell pepper.

Roasted vegetables make a flavorful salad. Tofu is added for protein, and then everything is tossed with a zesty herbed miso dressing for a satisfying one-dish meal that is perfect on a hot day.

FOR THE DRESSING

Process in a blender until smooth:

> ¼ cup olive oil
>
> 6 tablespoons minced fresh basil
>
> 3 tablespoons minced fresh parsley
>
> 2 tablespoons balsamic vinegar
>
> 2 tablespoons mellow white miso
>
> 1 clove garlic

FOR THE VEGETABLES AND TOFU

Preheat the oven to 450 degrees F, and oil an 11 x 17-inch baking sheet.

Toss together in a large bowl:

> 2 pounds small yellow squash and zucchini, cut into ½-inch-thick slices
>
> 3 small bell peppers (various colors), cut into 1-inch pieces
>
> 1 small onion, cut into 1-inch pieces
>
> 6 tablespoons chopped fresh basil
>
> 2 tablespoons olive oil
>
> 2 cloves garlic, minced or pressed

Arrange the vegetables in a single layer on the prepared baking sheet, and roast them in the oven for about 10 minutes, or until they are crisp-tender. Toss the hot vegetables in a large glass or stainless steel bowl with the prepared dressing.

Stir in:

> 1 pound firm tofu, cut into ½-inch cubes

Chill in the refrigerator for a few hours before serving to allow the flavors to blend. Serve on a bed of lettuce, and garnish with red or yellow cherry or pear tomatoes.

VARIATION

Roasted Vegetable Salad with Tofu and Pasta: Double the amount of dressing. Cook ½ pound pasta spirals, shells, or penne until just tender. Drain well and add the hot pasta to the roasted vegetables and tofu. Mix well. Chill and serve as directed.

Spanish Tofu Rice Salad

This tasty combination makes good use of leftover cooked rice.

Combine in a glass or stainless steel bowl:

- ½ pound firm regular tofu, cut into small cubes
- ¼ cup freshly squeezed lemon juice
- 1 teaspoon salt
- 1 clove garlic, pressed, or ½ teaspoon garlic powder

Cover and refrigerate for 30 minutes. Stir together in a separate large bowl:

- 4 cups cooked brown or white rice
- 2 ripe tomatoes, diced
- 3 green onions, chopped
- ¼ cup freshly squeezed lemon juice
- 2 tablespoons olive oil
- 1 green or poblano chile, diced
- 2 to 3 teaspoons salt

Stir the rice mixture and the tofu together, then chill in the refrigerator for 2 to 3 hours.

Just before serving, stir in:

- ¼ to ½ cup chopped fresh parsley or cilantro
- ⅛ teaspoon freshly ground black pepper

Tofu Lentil Salad

Curry powder spices up this hearty salad.

Have ready:

- 2 cups cooked or canned lentils, drained

FOR THE DRESSING

Stir, process, or shake together in a jar:

- 2 tablespoons olive oil
- 2 tablespoons apple cider vinegar
- 1 teaspoon curry powder
- ½ teaspoon salt
- ¼ teaspoon freshly ground black pepper

FOR THE SALAD

Combine the lentils and dressing in a large bowl with:

- ¾ pound firm regular tofu, crumbled
- ½ cup diced celery
- ½ cup grated carrot
- ¼ cup sweet pickle relish
- 2 tablespoons diced onion
- 1 teaspoon curry powder
- 1 teaspoon salt

Mix well. Chill thoroughly before serving.

Asian Slaw

Ginger, cilantro, mint, rice vinegar, and miso give this slaw a special twist. Asian Slaw is pictured on page 54.

FOR THE DRESSING

Chop in a blender or food processor:

> ¼ small sweet yellow onion
>
> ¼ cup fresh cilantro leaves, packed
>
> ¼ cup fresh mint leaves, packed
>
> 1 piece (½-inch cube) peeled fresh ginger
>
> 1 clove garlic

Add and process until smooth and creamy:

> ¼ pound soft regular tofu, mashed or crumbled (½ cup)
>
> 3 tablespoons rice vinegar
>
> 3 tablespoons sweetener of your choice
>
> 2 tablespoons light olive or peanut oil
>
> 2 tablespoons sweet white miso
>
> Dash of crushed red pepper flakes

FOR THE SALAD

Mix in a salad bowl:

> 3 cups shredded napa or green cabbage
>
> 1½ cups shredded carrot
>
> 1½ cups mung bean sprouts
>
> 1 cup shredded red cabbage or radicchio
>
> 1 cup minced kale leaves or fresh parsley

Stir the dressing into the salad. Serve topped with:

> 1 tablespoon toasted sesame seeds

Salad sans Poulet

Try this chicken-free salad stuffed in a pita bread, served as a salad on lettuce or mesclun, or in a sandwich.

Have ready:

> 1 pound firm regular tofu, frozen, thawed, squeezed dry, and chopped

Combine the tofu in a large bowl with:

> ⅓ cup minced onion
>
> ⅓ cup minced celery
>
> 1 tablespoon nutritional yeast flakes
>
> 1 tablespoon minced fresh parsley
>
> ½ teaspoon poultry seasoning
>
> 1 clove garlic, minced, or ½ teaspoon garlic powder
>
> ¼ teaspoon freshly ground black pepper

Stir in:

> 1½ cups Tofu Salad Dressing (page 50) or Tofu Aïoli (page 47)

Sprouted Lentil Salad

Enjoy the benefits of raw food, live food, and soyfood together! Sprouted lentils are relatively easy to grow at home.

Mix together in a small bowl:

2 tablespoons freshly squeezed lemon juice

2 tablespoons sweet white miso

1 tablespoon olive oil

Fold in:

½ pound firm regular tofu, cut into ⅛-inch cubes

Cover and let marinate in the refrigerator for 8 to 12 hours.

Mix together in a salad bowl:

2 cups sprouted lentils

1 cup peeled, seeded, and chopped cucumber

½ cup chopped green bell pepper

½ cup chopped yellow bell pepper

½ cup shredded carrot

½ cup grape tomatoes, sliced in half

¼ cup minced fresh mint or parsley

Fold in the marinated tofu and serve.

Picnic Potato Salad

For this salad, the potatoes absorb the seasonings while they are still hot.

FOR THE SALAD

Boil in salted water or steam until tender:

4 medium-size potatoes (about 2 pounds)

Drain the potatoes, pull off and discard the skins, cube the flesh, and place it in a large bowl. Combine in a small bowl, then mix with the hot potatoes:

1 tablespoon olive oil

1 tablespoon apple cider vinegar

½ teaspoon salt

⅛ teaspoon freshly ground black pepper

⅛ teaspoon dry mustard

Let the potatoes cool. Then stir in:

1 cup diced celery

⅓ cup minced onion

2 tablespoons minced fresh parsley

¼ teaspoon celery salt

FOR THE DRESSING

Process in a blender or food processor until smooth and creamy:

½ pound soft regular tofu, mashed or crumbled

2 tablespoons apple cider vinegar

Gently stir the dressing into the potatoes. Chill thoroughly before serving.

Note: Use insulated kitchen gloves to protect your hands while peeling and cubing the hot potatoes.

Cottage Tofu Salad

Serve this versatile mixture as a sandwich spread, dip, or salad on a bed of lettuce.

Stir together in a medium-size bowl:

> 1 pound firm regular tofu, mashed or crumbled
>
> 2 tablespoons minced fresh chives, or 1½ teaspoons dried
>
> 1 tablespoon minced fresh parsley
>
> 1 teaspoon minced fresh dill, or ¼ teaspoon dried

Process in a blender or food processor until smooth and creamy:

> ¼ pound soft regular tofu, mashed or crumbled (½ cup)

> 1½ teaspoons white wine vinegar or apple cider vinegar
>
> 1½ teaspoons freshly squeezed lemon juice
>
> 1 teaspoon salt
>
> ¼ to ½ teaspoon freshly ground black pepper

Pour into the tofu mixture and stir well.

Golden Tofu Salad

Serve this egg-free tofu salad as you would egg salad. Turmeric gives it a soft yellow color.

Stir together in a large bowl:

> 1 pound firm regular tofu, mashed or crumbled
>
> ½ cup Tofu Salad Dressing (page 50)
>
> ⅓ cup minced celery
>
> 1 tablespoon minced fresh parsley
>
> 2 teaspoons prepared yellow or Dijon mustard

> 1 teaspoon onion powder
>
> 1 teaspoon salt
>
> ½ teaspoon garlic powder
>
> ½ teaspoon freshly ground black pepper
>
> ½ teaspoon paprika
>
> ¼ teaspoon turmeric

Savory Tofu Salad

Tofu salad can be served as a sandwich spread or dip, scooped onto a bed of lettuce or tomato slices, or stuffed into a fresh bell pepper or ripe avocado.

Stir together in a large bowl:

1½ pounds firm regular tofu, mashed or crumbled

½ cup Tofu Salad Dressing (page 50)

½ cup chopped fresh parsley

½ medium-size onion, minced

2 stalks celery, minced

¼ cup sweet or dill pickle relish

1½ teaspoons garlic powder

1½ teaspoons salt

½ teaspoon paprika

¼ teaspoon freshly ground black pepper

Tabouli

Tofu boosts the protein in this classic tabouli, pictured on the opposite page. If you have a wheat allergy, try the Quinoa Tabouli variation that follows.

Combine and let soak for 1 hour:

2 cups boiling water

1 cup bulgur

Drain the bulgur well, transfer it to a large bowl, and mix in:

½ pound minced firm or extra-firm regular tofu

2 ripe tomatoes, chopped

1 cup minced fresh parsley

½ cup minced fresh mint

½ cup chopped black or kalamata olives

¼ cup freshly squeezed lemon juice

¼ cup chopped green onions

2 tablespoons olive oil

½ teaspoon salt

¼ teaspoon freshly ground black pepper

Serve on a bed of leaf lettuce garnished with additional tomato wedges.

VARIATION

Quinoa Tabouli: Omit the bulgur. Simmer 1 cup quinoa with 2 cups water in a covered pot for 20 minutes. Remove from the heat and let stand covered for 10 minutes. Fluff the quinoa with a fork before combining it with the other ingredients.

Cucumber Boats

Serve this tasty filling as a salad in cucumber boats, or turn it into finger sandwiches for an appetizer. Whichever version you choose, prepare it right before serving.

Peel, cut in half lengthwise, and remove the seeds from:

> 4 medium-size cucumbers

Mix together in a medium-size bowl:

> ½ pound firm regular tofu, mashed
>
> 6 tablespoons freshly squeezed lime juice
>
> ¼ cup minced onion
>
> 3 tablespoons white or yellow miso
>
> 2 tablespoons nutritional yeast flakes (optional)
>
> ½ teaspoon salt

Arrange the cucumber halves on a platter and fill them with the tofu mixture. Sprinkle the tops with chili powder just before serving.

VARIATION

Cucumber Finger Sandwiches: Score or peel the cucumbers and slice them into ¼-inch rounds. Place each slice on a round cracker, top with a dollop of the tofu mixture, and sprinkle with chili powder just before serving.

Tabouli

Potato Tofu Salad

This is vegan potato salad for a crowd.

FOR THE SALAD

Boil in salted water or steam until tender:

> 6 medium-size red or yellow potatoes, cubed (about 3 pounds)

Transfer the potatoes to a large mixing bowl and combine with:

> ½ pound firm regular tofu, crumbled
>
> 1 cup finely diced celery
>
> ½ cup minced red onion
>
> ½ cup sweet pickle relish
>
> 1½ teaspoons salt

FOR THE DRESSING

Process in a blender or food processor until smooth and creamy:

> ½ pound soft regular tofu, mashed or crumbled
>
> 1½ tablespoons apple cider vinegar
>
> 1 tablespoon prepared yellow mustard
>
> 1½ teaspoons freshly squeezed lemon juice
>
> ½ teaspoon salt
>
> 1 small clove garlic, pressed, or ¼ teaspoon garlic powder
>
> Dash of freshly ground black pepper

Gently mix the dressing into the potatoes and tofu. Chill thoroughly before serving.

Sesame Tofu Salad

Toasted sesame seeds add a special delicate flavor to this tofu salad.

Stir together in a medium-size bowl:

> 1 pound firm regular tofu, crumbled
>
> ¾ cup Tofu Salad Dressing (page 50)
>
> ⅓ cup minced onion
>
> ⅓ cup minced celery
>
> 2 tablespoons toasted sesame seeds
>
> 4 teaspoons dill pickle relish
>
> 2 teaspoons minced fresh dill, or ½ teaspoon dried
>
> 1 teaspoon salt

Cucumber-Tomato Salad

This creamy salad is great during summer when cucumbers and tomatoes are bountiful.

FOR THE SALAD

Mix together in a salad bowl:

    4 cups sliced cucumbers
    3 cups chopped tomatoes
    1 cup chopped celery
    ⅔ cup chopped onion
    ½ cup chopped fresh parsley

FOR THE DRESSING

Process in a blender or food processor until smooth and creamy:

    ½ pound soft regular tofu, mashed or crumbled
    3 tablespoons freshly squeezed lime juice
    1 tablespoon olive or walnut oil (optional)
    1 teaspoon sweetener of your choice
    ½ teaspoon salt
    ¼ teaspoon freshly ground black pepper

Combine the salad and dressing and mix well. Chill thoroughly before serving.

Lettuce Rolls

Use the large leaves of any variety of lettuce for these rolls. Different colored leaves make an appealing presentation. Make smaller rolls from smaller leaves for appetizers.

Combine in a medium-size bowl:

    1 pound firm regular tofu, mashed
    ½ cup sliced black olives
    3 green onions, minced
    2 stalks celery, minced
    ¼ cup sweet pickle relish (optional)

Stir in:

    1½ cups Tofu Salad Dressing (page 50)

Wash and dry the large outer leaves of 1 head of any kind of lettuce. Remove the stiff core section of the leaves. Place ¼ cup of the salad mixture along 1 side of each leaf and roll up. Cut each roll into 3-inch or bite-size sections and use toothpicks to keep them snug.

Kanten Fruit and Vegetable Salad

MAKES 6 TO 8 SERVINGS

Kanten gels can include either fruits or vegetables. This makes a very firm gel.

Place in a 3-quart saucepan and bring to a boil over medium-high heat:

> 3 cups apricot nectar
>
> 3 tablespoons agar flakes

Lower the heat and simmer, stirring often, for 5 minutes, or until dissolved. Set aside to cool.

Process in a blender or food processor until smooth and creamy:

> ½ pound soft regular tofu, mashed or crumbled

Stir the blended tofu into the cooled agar mixture along with:

> 1½ cups shredded carrots
>
> ¾ cup walnuts or pecans
>
> ½ cup golden raisins
>
> 3 tablespoons sweetener of your choice
>
> ½ teaspoon vanilla extract

Pour into a 6-cup dessert mold or individual serving dishes. Chill for 4 to 12 hours, or until firm. Remove from the mold before serving.

Apple-Nut Salad

MAKES 6 TO 8 SERVINGS

The creamy base for this classic salad is made with tofu.

Mix together in a large bowl:

> 4 tart red apples, chopped
>
> 2 cups diced celery
>
> ½ cup chopped pecans
>
> ¼ cup freshly squeezed lemon juice

Place in a small bowl or measuring cup:

> ½ cup raisins

Pour boiling water over the raisins to cover and let soak for about 15 minutes. Drain the raisins and stir them into the apple mixture along with:

> 1½ cups Tofu Sour Creamy Dressing (page 50)

Chill thoroughly before serving.

Creamy Apple Kanten Gel with Fruit

MAKES 6 TO 8 SERVINGS

Agar, also known as kanten, is a plant-based gelatin made from sea vegetables. It comes flaked or pow-dered, ready to be dissolved in hot liquid. This fruit gel can be served as a salad or a light dessert. Any combination of fruits can be enjoyed in season or from the freezer. Using frozen fruit causes the gel to become firm almost immediately.

Arrange in a 6-cup dessert mold:

> 1½ cups sliced bananas
>
> 1 cup blueberries
>
> ½ cup pitted cherries

Process in a blender or food processor until smooth and creamy:

> 3½ cups apple juice
>
> ½ pound soft regular tofu, mashed or crumbled
>
> ¼ cup sweetener of your choice (optional)
>
> ½ teaspoon ground cinnamon (optional)

Pour into a 2-quart saucepan and bring to a boil over medium-high heat. Reduce the heat to low and whisk in:

> 2 teaspoons agar powder

Simmer and stir with a whisk for 1 minute, until the agar is dissolved. Pour the hot liquid over the fruit in the mold. Chill until firm. Remove from the mold before serving.

VARIATION

To replace the agar powder with flakes, add 2 tablespoons agar flakes when processing the juice and tofu. Cook and stir for about 5 minutes, until the flakes are thoroughly dissolved. Pour the hot liquid over the fruit in the mold and chill until firm.

Frozen Fruit Salad

MAKES 6 TO 8 SERVINGS

This makes a cool, light meal or dessert for a hot day.

FOR THE DRESSING

Process in a blender or food processor until smooth and creamy:

> 1 pound soft regular tofu, mashed or crumbled
>
> ¼ cup sweetener of your choice
>
> ¼ cup freshly squeezed lemon juice
>
> 2 tablespoons canola or light olive oil
>
> ½ teaspoon salt

FOR THE SALAD

Mix in a large bowl:

> 4 cups drained fruit, fresh or canned
>
> ½ cup chopped pecans
>
> 2 teaspoons chopped crystallized ginger

Fold the dressing into the salad, spoon it into individual serving dishes, and freeze. Thaw for 15 minutes before serving.

Spring Quinoa Salad

Enjoy this salad full of spring vegetables either warm or chilled. Vary the vegetables according to your taste or what is available.

Simmer in a covered pot for 20 minutes:

> 2 cups boiling water
>
> 1 cup quinoa

Remove from the heat and let stand for 10 minutes. Fluff the quinoa with a fork. While the quinoa is cooking, heat in a large skillet or sauté pan over medium heat:

> 1 tablespoon olive oil

Add and cook and stir in the heated oil over medium-high heat just until crisp-tender (about 3 minutes):

> ½ pound asparagus, trimmed and cut on the diagonal into 1-inch pieces
>
> ½ cup thinly sliced carrots, cut on the diagonal
>
> ¼ pound sugar snap peas or snow peas, cut on the diagonal into 1-inch pieces

Sprinkle the cooked vegetables with:

> 1 tablespoon soy sauce

Stir the cooked vegetables into the quinoa along with:

> 1 cup Tofu Salad Dressing (page 50) or Aïoli Dressing (page 47)
>
> ½ cup thinly sliced celery, cut on the diagonal
>
> ¼ cup thinly sliced green onions, cut on the diagonal

Season with salt and pepper to taste.

Salad Dressings and Sauces

With so many types of prewashed greens available, you can prepare a quick, creamy tofu dressing and have a side salad ready in a snap. Even slaw vegetables are available preshredded and need only a hearty tofu dressing to swiftly turn them into a vegan side dish.

Tofu-based salad dressings and sauces turn out best when very fresh extra-soft regular tofu, aseptically packaged silken tofu, or traditional soft Japanese-style silken tofu is used (see Processing or Blending Tofu, page 4). If you are calorie conscious, just leave the oil out of any recipe; you'll still have a creamy and delicious dressing or sauce. For an extra boost of omega-3 and omega-6 fatty acids, use flaxseed oil, hempseed oil, or chia seed oil in recipes that don't require cooking.

Creamy Sweet-and-Sour Poppy Seed Fruit Salad Dressing

Tahini Tofu Lemon Sauce

Pour this special sauce on Falafel (page 98) or steamed vegetables.

Chop in a food processor or blender:

1 to 3 cloves garlic

Add and process until smooth and creamy:

½ cup tahini

½ pound firm regular tofu, mashed or crumbled

¼ cup freshly squeezed lemon juice

½ teaspoon salt, or 1½ teaspoons mellow white miso

Pour into a bowl and stir in:

2 tablespoons minced fresh lemon balm (optional)

Thousand Island Dressing

Process in a blender or food processor until smooth and creamy:

½ pound soft regular tofu, mashed or crumbled

½ cup ketchup

2 tablespoons olive oil (optional)

½ teaspoon onion powder

¼ teaspoon salt

1 small clove garlic, minced or pressed, or ¼ teaspoon garlic powder

Pour into a bowl. Then stir in:

3 tablespoons sweet pickle relish

3 tablespoons minced pimiento-stuffed green olives

1 tablespoon minced fresh parsley

Creamy Italian Dressing

Process in a blender or food processor until smooth and creamy:

½ pound soft regular tofu, mashed or crumbled

2 tablespoons olive oil (optional)

2 tablespoons white wine vinegar

1 teaspoon salt

⅛ teaspoon freshly ground black pepper

Pour into a bowl and stir in:

2 tablespoons sweet pickle relish (optional)

2 to 4 cloves garlic, minced or pressed

1½ teaspoons minced fresh oregano, or ¼ teaspoon dried

⅛ teaspoon crushed red pepper flakes

Avocado Salad Dressing

MAKES 1¼ CUPS

Process in a blender or food processor until smooth and creamy:

- ½ cup Tofu Salad Dressing (page 50)
- 1 ripe avocado, mashed
- 1 tablespoon freshly squeezed lemon juice
- ½ teaspoon salt
- 1 small clove garlic, minced or pressed, or ½ teaspoon garlic powder
- ⅛ teaspoon freshly ground black pepper

Dill Salad Dressing

MAKES 1¼ CUPS

Process in a blender or food processor until smooth and creamy:

- ½ pound soft regular tofu, mashed or crumbled
- 1 tablespoon olive oil (optional)
- 1 tablespoon white wine vinegar or apple cider vinegar
- 1 tablespoon fresh minced dill, or ½ teaspoon dried
- ½ teaspoon salt
- ⅛ teaspoon freshly ground black pepper

Tofu Aïoli

MAKES ABOUT 2 CUPS

This is a vegan version of the French garlic mayonnaise classically served with seafood. Enjoy it with roasted potatoes, dark leafy greens, green beans, and other vegetables.

Chop in a food processor as finely as possible, or press with a garlic press into the bowl of a food processor:

- 6 to 7 large garlic cloves, peeled

Add and process into a paste:

- ½ teaspoon salt

Add and process until smooth and creamy:

- ½ pound soft tofu, mashed or crumbled
- ¼ cup olive oil

- 1 tablespoon freshly squeezed lemon juice
- 1 tablespoon Dijon mustard (optional)
- ¼ teaspoon freshly ground white pepper

With the food processor running, drizzle in through the cap opening:

- ¾ cup olive oil

Note: Remove any green sprouts from the middle of the garlic cloves for a more mellow garlic flavor.

Cucumber Salad Dressing

MAKES 1¾ CUPS

Process in a blender or food processor until smooth and creamy:

  ½ pound soft regular tofu, mashed or crumbled

  1 medium-size cucumber, peeled, seeded, and coarsely chopped

  2 tablespoons olive oil (optional)

2 tablespoons white wine vinegar or apple cider vinegar

½ teaspoon salt

⅛ teaspoon freshly ground black pepper

Green Goddess Dressing

MAKES 1¾ CUPS

This is a San Francisco favorite with salad greens and avocado.

Process in a blender or food processor until smooth and creamy:

  ½ pound soft regular tofu, mashed or crumbled

  ¼ cup minced fresh parsley

  2 tablespoons minced fresh chives, or 1½ teaspoons dried

  2 tablespoons olive oil (optional)

2 tablespoons freshly squeezed lemon juice or tarragon vinegar

1 teaspoon onion powder

½ teaspoon salt

1 small clove garlic, minced or pressed, or ¼ teaspoon garlic powder

⅛ teaspoon freshly ground black pepper

Russian Dressing

MAKES 1½ CUPS

Process in a blender or food processor until smooth and creamy:

  ½ pound soft regular tofu, mashed or crumbled

  ⅓ cup ketchup

  2 tablespoons white wine vinegar or freshly squeezed lemon juice

2 tablespoons olive oil (optional)

1 tablespoon prepared yellow mustard

1 teaspoon onion powder

½ teaspoon salt

CREAMY SWEET-AND-SOUR POPPY SEED Fruit Salad Dressing

MAKES ABOUT 2 CUPS

This recipe is pictured on page 45.

Process in a blender or food processor until smooth and creamy:

¼ pound soft regular tofu, mashed or crumbled (½ cup)

½ cup apple cider vinegar

⅓ cup sweetener of your choice

2 tablespoons olive oil (optional)

2 tablespoons minced onion

2 tablespoons poppy seeds

1½ teaspoons dry mustard

1 teaspoon salt

1 teaspoon paprika

SWEET-AND-SPICY Fruit Salad Dressing

MAKES 1¾ CUPS

Process in a blender or food processor until smooth and creamy:

½ pound soft regular tofu, mashed or crumbled

¼ cup freshly squeezed lemon juice

¼ cup sweetener of your choice

2 tablespoons olive oil (optional)

¼ teaspoon ground cinnamon

¼ teaspoon vanilla extract

⅛ teaspoon salt

Lemon-Caper Dressing

MAKES ABOUT 1¼ CUPS

Process in a blender until smooth and creamy:

½ pound soft regular tofu, mashed or crumbled

2 tablespoons freshly squeezed lemon juice

1 tablespoon sweetener of your choice

½ teaspoon salt

Pour into a bowl. Then stir in:

6 tablespoons capers

Tofu Sour Creamy Dressing

This is a versatile recipe you will turn to again and again. Use it just like dairy sour cream.

Process in a blender or food processor until smooth and creamy:

½ pound soft regular tofu, mashed or crumbled

2 tablespoons olive oil (optional)

1 tablespoon freshly squeezed lemon juice

1½ teaspoons sweetener of your choice

½ teaspoon salt

Tofu Salad Dressing

Enjoy this basic creamy dressing in place of mayonnaise for salads and sandwiches.

Process in a blender or food processor until smooth and creamy:

½ pound soft regular tofu, mashed or crumbled

2 tablespoons olive oil (optional)

2 tablespoons apple cider vinegar or freshly squeezed lemon juice

1 tablespoon sweetener of your choice

½ teaspoon salt

Note: If you are using a firmer tofu, you may need to add a little water to facilitate processing.

Tartar Sauce

Process in a blender or food processor until smooth and creamy:

½ pound soft regular tofu, mashed or crumbled

¼ cup white wine vinegar or freshly squeezed lemon juice

2 tablespoons olive oil (optional)

2 tablespoons sweetener of your choice

1 teaspoon prepared yellow mustard

¾ teaspoon salt

Pour into a bowl and stir in:

½ cup chopped onion

¼ cup sweet pickle relish

Hollandaise Sauce

Process in a blender or food processor until smooth and creamy:

½ pound soft regular tofu, mashed or crumbled

¼ cup olive oil

¼ cup freshly squeezed lemon juice

½ teaspoon sweetener of your choice

½ teaspoon salt

⅛ teaspoon freshly ground black pepper

Dash of cayenne

Note: This sauce may be heated and served hot, but be careful not to let it boil.

Horseradish Sauce

Process in a blender or food processor until smooth and creamy:

¼ pound soft regular tofu, mashed or crumbled (½ cup)

3 tablespoons prepared horseradish

1 tablespoon olive oil (optional)

1 tablespoon white wine vinegar or freshly squeezed lemon juice

1 teaspoon sweetener of your choice

½ teaspoon salt

Silken Miso Sauce

This can be served hot or cold over vegetables, grains, or pasta.

Process in a blender or food processor until smooth and creamy:

1 package (12.3 ounces) silken tofu, mashed or crumbled

3 tablespoons apple cider vinegar

2 tablespoons sweet white or yellow miso

2 tablespoons olive oil (optional)

1 teaspoon sweetener of your choice

1 small clove garlic, minced or pressed, or ¼ teaspoon garlic powder

¼ teaspoon freshly ground black pepper

Note: This sauce may be heated and served hot, but be careful not to let it boil.

Korean Barbecued Tofu, page 56

main

Main Dishes

4

Versatile tofu takes on so many shapes, forms, textures, and flavors for main dishes. It is not just for stir-fries! As a high-protein staple that absorbs and showcases whatever flavors are added to it, tofu can take the place of meat and similar animal-based foods in any conventional dish. Many ethnic dishes lend themselves well to incorporating tofu. Firm and extra-firm tofu work best in dishes where it's important for the tofu to retain its shape. Frozen tofu offers the most chewy texture and provides maximum absorption of flavorings. Tofu also does an excellent job of standing in for ricotta in dishes like lasagne.

These recipes are for tofu that is flavored in various ways but stands on its own to occupy the center of the plate. It takes the form of slices, cubes, pieces, cutlets, nuggets, or sticks, or it may be scrambled or pressed into a loaf. Fill the rest of the plate with side dishes of vegetables, whole grains, breads, or tortillas, as suggested or as you like.

Barbecued Tofu. page 55 and Asian Slaw, page 35

Frozen tofu lends a chewy texture to this barbecued dish. Try cooking it on the grill, covered with aluminum foil to prevent the sauce from escaping. This recipe is pictured on the opposite page.

FOR THE TOFU

Cut into 1 x ½-inch-thick strips:

> 2 pounds firm to extra-firm tofu, frozen, thawed, and squeezed dry

Preheat the oven to 350 degrees F, and generously oil an 11 x 17-inch jelly roll pan with olive oil. Arrange the tofu strips on the prepared baking sheet. Mix together by hand or in a blender:

> ¼ cup water
>
> 2 tablespoons natural peanut butter
>
> 1 tablespoon soy sauce
>
> 1 clove garlic, pressed, or ½ teaspoon garlic powder
>
> ¼ teaspoon freshly ground black pepper

Pour evenly over the tofu strips and press the mixture into them with a spatula or the palm of your hand (see Freezing Tofu, page 4). Bake for about 15 minutes, then turn the pieces over and bake for about 10 minutes longer, or until lightly browned.

Pour about 4 cups of your favorite barbecue sauce (or use the recipe that follows) evenly over the tofu and bake for 10 minutes longer. Serve with French bread and your favorite green salad or slaw.

FOR THE BARBEQUE SAUCE

Heat in a 2-quart saucepan over low heat:

> 2 tablespoons olive oil

Cook and stir in the heated oil over medium heat until transparent:

> 1 medium-size onion, chopped
>
> 2 cloves garlic, minced

Stir in:

> 1 can (15 ounces) tomato sauce
>
> ¾ cup brown sugar or sweetener of your choice
>
> ½ cup prepared yellow mustard
>
> ½ cup water
>
> 1 tablespoon molasses
>
> 1 tablespoon chopped fresh parsley, or 1½ teaspoons dried
>
> 1 teaspoon ground allspice
>
> 1 teaspoon crushed red pepper flakes, or ½ teaspoon cayenne

Bring to a boil, lower the heat, and stir in:

> ½ cup freshly squeezed lemon juice or apple cider vinegar
>
> 2 tablespoons soy sauce

Simmer for 10 to 15 minutes.

Korean Barbecued Tofu

Korean barbecue sauce imparts a special flavor to this tofu. A square-shaped skillet will make it easier to fit in and cook the tofu slices. Serve the tofu over rice or rice noodles, garnished with chopped green onions, mushrooms, and/or snow peas (see photo, page 52).

Cut into ¼-inch slices and arrange in a single layer in a 9 x 13-inch glass or stainless steel pan:

> 1½ pounds firm or extra-firm regular tofu

To make the marinade, stir together:

> ½ cup soy sauce
>
> 6 tablespoons sweetener of your choice
>
> 1 tablespoon grated onion, or 2 teaspoons onion powder
>
> 2 teaspoons dry mustard

> 4 cloves garlic, minced or pressed, or
> 2 teaspoons garlic powder

Cover and let marinate in the refrigerator for 2 to 12 hours (the longer it marinates, the more flavor it will absorb).

Heat in a large skillet or sauté pan over low heat:

> 2 tablespoons canola or light olive oil

Add the tofu slices and brown them on both sides over medium heat.

Marinating Korean Barbecued Tofu with the help of a baster

Apricot-Orange Barbecue

Use either fresh or frozen tofu for this dish; frozen tofu makes a chewier version.

FOR THE TOFU

Preheat the oven to 350 degrees F. Cut into ¼-inch-thick slices:

   1 pound firm or extra-firm regular tofu

Heat in a large skillet over low heat:

   1 tablespoon olive oil

Lightly fry the tofu slices in the heated oil, then arrange them in a single layer in a 7 x 11-inch baking dish.

Heat in a medium-size skillet or sauté pan over low heat:

   1 tablespoon olive oil

Cook and stir in the heated oil over medium heat until transparent:

   ¼ cup minced onion

FOR THE SAUCE

Stir into the cooked onions:

   6 tablespoons apricot jam

   5 tablespoons frozen orange juice concentrate and 5 tablespoons water, or 10 tablespoons orange juice

   2 tablespoons prepared yellow mustard

   1 tablespoon apple cider vinegar

   1 to 1½ teaspoons grated fresh ginger

   ½ teaspoon ground coriander

   ½ teaspoon ground fenugreek (optional)

   ½ teaspoon salt

   1 clove garlic, minced or pressed

   ⅛ teaspoon cayenne (optional)

Pour the sauce over the tofu and bake for 10 to 15 minutes, or until bubbling.

VARIATION

Chewy Apricot-Orange Barbecue: For a chewier version, use frozen tofu that has been thawed and gently squeezed dry. Cut the tofu into ¼-inch-thick slices or sticks and arrange them in a lightly oiled 7 x 11-inch baking dish. Pour the sauce over the tofu and gently press down with a spatula or the palm of your hand to allow the sauce to be absorbed into the tofu (see Freezing Tofu, page 4). Bake as directed.

Chewy Tofu Nuggets

Frozen tofu gives these nuggets their chewy texture. Serve them along with stir-fried veggies or a salad. They make a protein-packed snack as well as a great appetizer (serve them with toothpicks).

Preheat the oven to 350 degrees F, and oil an 11 x 17-inch baking sheet.

Have ready:

> 1 pound firm to extra-firm regular tofu, frozen, thawed, and squeezed dry

Tear the tofu into 1- to 1½-inch chunks and place them in a bowl.

Process in a small food processor or blender:

> ¼ cup water
>
> 2 tablespoons soy sauce
>
> 2 tablespoons almond butter or natural peanut butter

> 1 clove garlic, or ½ teaspoon garlic powder

Pour over the tofu and carefully squeeze the sauce into it by gently pressing down with a spatula or the palm of your hand and letting go until it is evenly distributed, taking care to not break up the tofu pieces (see Freezing Tofu, page 4). Spread the pieces in a single layer on the prepared baking sheet and bake for about 10 minutes, or until they start to brown. Flip the pieces over and bake for 5 to 10 minutes longer, or until browned on both sides. Serve hot or warm.

Sesame Tofu

The delicate flavor of sesame enhances these baked tofu slices.

Preheat the oven to 350 degrees F, and generously oil an 11 x 17-inch baking sheet with olive oil. Cut into ¾-inch cubes or ¼-inch-thick slices:

> 1 pound firm to extra-firm regular tofu

To make the dry coating, grind together in a food processor, and then pour into a bowl:

> ⅓ cup sesame seeds
>
> ⅓ cup unbleached flour

To make the sauce, chop in a food processor:

> 1 piece (1-inch cube) peeled fresh ginger
>
> 2 cloves garlic

Add and process until well combined:

> 2 tablespoons soy sauce
>
> 2 tablespoons water

Pour the sauce into a bowl. Use one hand to first dip each piece of tofu into the sauce, and keep the other hand dry to then dredge the tofu with the sesame mixture. Arrange the coated slices on the prepared baking sheet.

Sprinkle any leftover sauce over the slices, then sprinkle on any leftover sesame mixture. Bake for 20 minutes, then turn the slices over and bake for 10 minutes longer. Serve hot with rice and steamed vegetables.

Chile Colorado

This is an adaptation of a northern Mexican dish. Frozen tofu is used in place of the traditional beef; it imparts a similar tender and chewy texture and soaks up the flavorful chile sauce. The type of chiles that are typically used for this recipe vary depending on the region and family tradition. Start with dried whole chiles with no blemishes or tears. A comal is the Mexican version of a griddle and can be made of metal or clay. Serve Chile Colorado with flour or corn tortillas, chopped white onions, and fresh cilantro.

Have ready:

> 2 pounds firm regular tofu, frozen, thawed, and squeezed dry
>
> 4 dried whole guajillo, California, or New Mexico chiles, rinsed
>
> 4 dried whole ancho chiles

Tear the tofu into bite-size pieces. Slit the chiles down one side and remove the stems, seeds, and membranes. Open up the chiles and toast them on a griddle or *comal* over medium-high heat for a few minutes. (Pressing the chiles down with a spatula, just until they start to bubble, will help speed up the process.) Toast the chiles inside and out, and don't let them burn—burning gives them a bitter flavor.

Place the toasted chiles in a 2-quart saucepan or bowl, cover them with boiling water, and let them soak for about 30 minutes. Remove the chiles with a slotted spoon and transfer them to a blender with the some of the soaking water (if it is not bitter) or fresh water to cover. Process until smooth.

Heat in a 2-quart pot over low heat:

> ¼ cup canola oil

Cook and stir in the heated oil over medium heat until soft:

> 1 medium-size onion, minced
>
> 2 cloves of garlic, finely diced

Pour the blended chiles through a strainer into the pot with the cooked onions and garlic. Discard any larger pieces of the skins caught in the strainer. Add to the pot and bring to a simmer:

> 1 can (15 ounces) tomato sauce
>
> 1 tablespoon dried oregano
>
> 1 teaspoon ground cumin
>
> 1 teaspoon salt

Stir in the tofu and simmer for at least 15 minutes to let the flavors blend. Serve hot with flour or corn tortillas.

Five-Spice Tofu

MAKES 4 TO 6 SERVINGS

Five-spice powder is a combination of ground spices, usually consisting of equal parts cinnamon, cloves, fennel seed, star anise, and Szechuan peppercorns. It is used extensively in Chinese cooking and can be found in Asian markets and most supermarkets.

To make the marinade, chop in a food processor or blender:

- 1 piece (½-inch cube) peeled fresh ginger
- 1 small jalapeño chile
- 2 cloves garlic

Add and process until combined:

- 2 tablespoons rice vinegar
- 2 tablespoons soy sauce
- 2 teaspoons five-spice powder

Cut into 10 equal slices:

- 1 pound firm regular tofu

Arrange the tofu slices in a single layer in a 9 x 13-inch glass or stainless steel pan. Pour the marinade over the tofu, cover, and place in the refrigerator for 8 to 12 hours, turning the pieces over several times.

Brown the marinated tofu in olive oil. Serve with rice and stir-fried vegetables.

Note: For a milder dish, remove the seeds and membranes from the chile and reduce the amount of fresh ginger. It's a good idea to wear kitchen gloves when working with hot chiles, and remember to never touch your eyes, mouth, or skin, as the oils from the chiles will sting and burn.

Indonesian Satay

MAKES 4 TO 6 SERVINGS

Spicy peanut sauce infuses flavor into the tofu for this Indonesian treat.

To make the sauce, chop in a food processor:

- 1 piece (1-inch cube) peeled fresh ginger
- 2 cloves garlic

Add and process until smooth:

- ¼ cup boiling water
- 2 tablespoons soy sauce
- 2 tablespoons natural peanut butter
- 2 teaspoons sweetener of your choice
- ½ teaspoon ground coriander
- ½ teaspoon rice vinegar or freshly squeezed lemon juice
- ⅛ teaspoon cayenne

Cut into ½-inch-thick slices:

- 1 pound firm to extra-firm regular tofu

Generously oil the bottom of an 8-inch square baking pan with olive oil. Pour a thin layer of the sauce into the pan, and arrange the tofu slices over the sauce in a single layer. Pour the remaining sauce over the tofu. Cover and place in the refrigerator for at least 1 hour.

Preheat the oven to 375 degrees F. Bake the tofu for 20 to 25 minutes. Serve with rice and stir-fried or steamed vegetables.

Tofu Loaf

Wheat germ or ground flaxseeds take the place of eggs to bind this loaf together. Try it sliced and fried for sandwiches the next day. Tofu Loaf is pictured below.

Preheat the oven to 350 degrees F, and generously oil a standard loaf pan with olive oil.

Mix together in a large bowl:

> 1 pound firm to extra-firm regular tofu, mashed
>
> ½ cup wheat germ, or 2 tablespoons ground flaxseeds
>
> ⅓ cup minced fresh parsley
>
> ¼ cup chopped onion, or 1 tablespoon onion powder
>
> 2 tablespoons soy sauce
>
> 2 tablespoons nutritional yeast flakes (optional)
>
> 1½ teaspoons Dijon mustard
>
> 1 clove garlic, minced or pressed, or ½ teaspoon garlic powder
>
> ¼ teaspoon freshly ground black pepper

Press the tofu mixture into the prepared loaf pan and bake for about 1 hour. Let cool for at least 15 minutes before removing from the pan. Garnish with ketchup and fresh parsley or chopped arugula.

Tofu Loaf

Tofu Paprikash

This creamy, savory dish is based on an old Hungarian favorite.

Cut into ½-inch-thick slices:

> 1 pound firm to extra-firm regular tofu

Heat in a large skillet or sauté pan over low heat:

> 1 tablespoon olive oil

Lightly fry the tofu slices in the heated oil. While the tofu is frying, sprinkle it with:

> ½ teaspoon garlic powder (¼ teaspoon for each side)

Remove the tofu from pan and set aside. Add to the same pan and heat over low heat:

> 1 tablespoon olive oil

Add and cook and stir until the onions are lightly browned:

> 4 cups thinly sliced onions
>
> ½ teaspoon salt

Sprinkle the browned onions with:

> 1½ tablespoons paprika

Then pour in:

> 1 cup vegetable broth or water

Cover the pan and simmer for 10 minutes. Then stir in:

> 1 cup Tofu Sour Creamy Dressing (page 50)

Remove half of the sauce from the pan and arrange the reserved tofu in the pan in a single layer. Pour or spoon the rest of the sauce over the tofu and heat until simmering but not boiling. Serve on rice, noodles, or mashed potatoes.

Sweet-and-Sour Tofu

These tofu bites, with their crispy coating, make a great main dish with stir-fried or steamed vegetables on the side.

Cut into ½-inch cubes:

> 1 pound firm to extra-firm regular tofu

Coat the cubes in a mixture of:

> ½ cup cornstarch, or ¼ cup cornstarch and ¼ cup unbleached flour
>
> ¼ cup vegetable broth or water
>
> 2 tablespoons soy sauce

Deep-fry the coated cubes in canola oil heated to 365 to 368 degrees F, making sure the cubes remain separated in the oil. Cook for 2 to 3 minutes, or until golden brown. Remove the cubes from the oil with a slotted spoon and drain them on absorbent paper. Serve with Sweet-and-Sour Sauce, page 92.

These sandwiches are made with roasted eggplant slices in place of bread.

FOR THE EGGPLANT

Preheat the oven to 350 degrees F, and oil an 11 x 17-inch baking sheet.

Peel and cut into 12 to 16 slices (each about ½ inch thick):

   1 medium-size eggplant

Arrange the slices on paper towels and sprinkle with:

   1 teaspoon salt

Let sit for about 10 minutes, then wipe the salt off with a fresh paper towel.

To make the breading mixture, combine in a bowl:

   ¼ cup unbleached or whole wheat pastry flour

   ¼ cup cornmeal

   1½ teaspoons minced fresh oregano, or ½ teaspoon dried

   ¼ teaspoon garlic powder

   Dash of freshly ground black pepper

Dredge the eggplant slices in the breading mixture and place them in a single layer on the prepared baking sheet.

Bake for 8 to 10 minutes. Carefully flip the eggplant slices over while spreading on the baking sheet:

   1 tablespoon olive oil

Bake for 8 to 10 minutes longer, or until the eggplant is soft and browned.

FOR THE FILLING

While the eggplant is baking, mix together:

   1 pound firm regular tofu, mashed

   3 tablespoons freshly squeezed lemon juice

   2 tablespoons minced onion, or 1½ teaspoons onion powder

   1 to 2 tablespoons minced fresh basil, or 1 teaspoon dried

   1½ teaspoons sweetener of your choice

   ½ teaspoon salt

   1 clove garlic, minced or pressed, or ½ teaspoon garlic powder

PUTTING IT ALL TOGETHER

Spread half of the eggplant slices with about ⅓ cup of the filling. Place 1 slice of ripe tomato and some fresh sprouts (any kind; my favorite for this sandwich is alfalfa sprouts) over the filling, and top with a second eggplant slice. Serve with a knife and fork.

Note: The eggplant slices can be roasted without the breading, either on a hot grill or in the oven.

Basic Fried Tofu

You can create countless variations of this recipe just by substituting different herbs and flavorings to suit your taste. A square frying pan will come in handy, because the sliced tofu will fit into it nicely. This is a children's favorite when made without the garlic.

Cut into ¼- to ½-inch-thick slices (12 to 15 slices):

> 1½ pounds firm to extra-firm regular tofu

Heat in a skillet or sauté pan over medium heat:

> 1 tablespoon olive oil

Lightly brown the tofu slices in the heated oil and sprinkle with:

> 2 tablespoons soy sauce, or 1 teaspoon salt
> 1 to 2 tablespoons nutritional yeast flakes
> ¼ teaspoon garlic powder

When the tofu has browned on one side, flip it over and brown the other side. Serve hot as a main dish, in a sandwich or tortilla, or as a hearty snack.

VARIATIONS

Herbed Fried Tofu: While the tofu is cooking, sprinkle it with your favorite combination of fresh or dried herbs.

Vegemite, Marmite, or Miso Tofu: Omit the nutritional yeast and soy sauce or salt, and spread the tofu slices with Vegemite, Marmite, or miso to taste before browning them in the heated oil.

Breaded Fried Tofu: Omit the nutritional yeast flakes and garlic. Dip the tofu slices in the soy sauce. Then dredge them in the flour mixture used for Oven-Fried Tofu (page 65), and brown them in the heated oil.

Scrambled Tofu

This makes a quick, satisfying breakfast dish, or a hearty, hot protein dish for any meal.

Heat in a large skillet or sauté pan over low heat:

> 1 tablespoon olive oil

Cook and stir in the heated oil over low heat until tender:

> ½ cup chopped onion
> 1 clove garlic, minced or pressed, or ½ teaspoon garlic powder

Stir in:

> 1 pound soft or firm regular tofu, crumbled
> 1 tablespoon soy sauce
> 1 tablespoon nutritional yeast flakes (optional)
> 1 tablespoon minced fresh basil, or 1 teaspoon dried
> ¼ teaspoon freshly ground black pepper

Cook and stir until the tofu is heated through and starts to brown. Serve hot with toast or tortillas, or a side of a whole grain, such as brown rice or quinoa.

VARIATION

Chipotle Scramble: Omit the basil and pepper and add ¼ cup minced fresh cilantro and chipotle chili powder to taste.

Oven-Fried Tofu

This is one of my favorite quick and easy recipes for both children and adults. If you prefer, the tofu can be pan-fried on the stovetop rather than oven-fried.

Preheat the oven to 350 degrees F, and generously oil an 11 x 17-inch baking sheet with olive oil.

Cut into ¼- to ½-inch-thick slices:

    2 pounds firm regular tofu

Mix together in a medium-size bowl:

    1¼ cups unbleached or whole wheat pastry flour
    ¼ cup nutritional yeast flakes
    2 tablespoons onion powder
    1 tablespoon dried parsley flakes

Mix in another medium-size bowl:

    2 tablespoons soy sauce

    2 teaspoons garlic powder
    1 teaspoon poultry seasoning
    ½ teaspoon freshly ground black pepper

Use one hand to dip a tofu slice into the soy sauce mixture on both sides, then with your other (dry) hand, dredge the slice in the flour mixture. Arrange the coated slices on the prepared baking sheet and bake for 20 minutes. Flip the slices over and bake for 15 minutes longer, or until both sides are golden brown. If necessary, add a little more oil to the baking sheet for the second side. Serve hot or cold as a main dish, in sandwiches, or as a snack.

Crunchy Tofu Cutlets or Sticks

These can be made with either fresh or frozen tofu. Frozen tofu will make chewier cutlets or sticks.

Have ready:

    2 pounds firm to extra-firm fresh or frozen regular tofu (if frozen, thaw and gently squeeze dry)

Cut the tofu into 1½ x 3 x ¾-inch pieces and place in a single layer in a 9 x 13-inch glass or stainless steel baking pan. Pour over the top:

    ¼ cup soy sauce

Cover and marinate in the refrigerator for at least 2 hours.

Preheat the oven to 400 degrees F, and generously oil an 11 x 17-inch baking sheet with olive oil.

To make the coating, combine in a bowl:

    1 cup cracker crumbs
    1 cup unbleached flour
    2 teaspoons dried parsley flakes
    1 teaspoon salt
    1 teaspoon garlic powder
    ½ teaspoon turmeric

Roll the tofu pieces in the coating, and then arrange them in a single layer on the prepared baking sheet, leaving about ½ inch between the pieces. Bake for 15 minutes on each side, or until golden brown. Serve with Tartar Sauce (page 50) or cocktail sauce.

Tofu with Squash Blossoms AND BASIL OR CILANTRO

Fresh squash blossoms can be found in Latin American specialty markets, or if you have squash of any kind growing, pick the male flowers (the ones that have no squash attached to them) to use in cooking.

Heat in a large skillet or sauté pan over low heat:

> 1 tablespoon olive oil

Cook and stir together in the heated oil over low heat until soft:

> 1 medium-size onion, minced
>
> 1 small jalapeño chile, minced
>
> 1 clove garlic, minced

Add and cook and stir for about 2 minutes:

> 1 bunch squash blossoms (about 20), coarsely chopped
>
> 3 tablespoons chopped fresh basil or cilantro

Stir in and cook until heated:

> 1 pound firm regular tofu, mashed or crumbled

Serve hot as a filling for burritos, or serve on a plate with corn tortillas on the side.

VARIATION

Stuffed Squash Blossoms: Stuff additional whole squash blossoms with the filling, then gently brown them in olive oil.

Teriyaki Tofu

This dish uses a classic Japanese flavoring for tofu.

Cut into ¼-inch-thick slices (6 to 10 slices):

> 1 pound firm or extra-firm regular tofu

Arrange the slices in a single layer in a 7 x 11-inch glass or stainless steel pan.

To make the marinade, combine in a bowl:

> 1 small onion, minced
>
> 2 tablespoons soy sauce
>
> 1 tablespoon minced fresh ginger
>
> 1 tablespoon rice vinegar or freshly squeezed lemon juice
>
> 1 teaspoon sweetener of your choice
>
> 1 clove garlic, minced or pressed

Pour the marinade over the tofu, cover, and let marinate in the refrigerator for at least 2 hours. Drain and reserve the marinade.

Dip the tofu slices in a mixture of:

> ¼ cup unbleached flour or cornstarch
>
> ¼ teaspoon freshly ground black pepper

Heat in a skillet or sauté pan over medium heat:

> 2 tablespoons canola or olive oil

Brown the floured tofu slices on both sides in the heated oil. Lower the heat, pour in the reserved marinade, and simmer until it is absorbed, about 5 minutes.

Casseroles, Savory Pies, and One-Pot Dishes

Tofu handily takes the place of meat and eggs in these familiar dishes, which are always good for feeding a crowd and preparing in advance. Many of these recipes are old family favorites and are derived from various ethnic cuisines. If there are any leftovers, freeze them in individual portions for future meals.

Quiche, page 68

Quiche

This is a hearty, egg-free quiche for real men and anyone else who might be inclined to dig in and enjoy it. Quiche is pictured on page 67.

Have ready:

> 1 (8-inch) pie crust, unbaked

Preheat the oven to 350 degrees F. To prepare the filling, heat in a large skillet or sauté pan over medium heat:

> 2 tablespoons olive oil

Cook and stir in the heated oil until soft:

> 1 medium-size onion, chopped

Place in a bowl and mix:

> 1½ pounds firm regular tofu, mashed
> ¼ cup nutritional yeast flakes (optional)
> 3 tablespoons freshly squeezed lemon juice
> 2 tablespoons soy sauce
> 1 tablespoon dry mustard

> 1 clove garlic, minced or pressed, or ½ teaspoon garlic powder
> ¼ teaspoon freshly ground black pepper

Add the cooked onion and mix well. Spoon the tofu mixture into the pie crust and spread it out evenly. Bake for 45 to 60 minutes, or until it is set and lightly browned on top.

VARIATION

Tofu Quiche with Tempeh or Soy Bacon Bits: Cover the bottom of the unbaked pie crust with ¾ cup crumbled tempeh that has been fried in oil and drained on absorbent paper, or ½ cup soy-based imitation bacon bits. Spoon the tofu mixture on top, spread it out evenly, and bake as directed.

Potato Tofu Casserole

This can be a hearty, one-dish meal, or serve it with your favorite salad.

Preheat the oven to 325 degrees F, and oil an 8-inch square baking dish.

Mix together in a large bowl:

> 3 cups mashed potatoes
> 1½ pounds firm regular tofu, mashed
> ¼ cup chopped fresh parsley
> 1¼ teaspoons salt
> ¼ teaspoon freshly ground black pepper
> 1 clove garlic, minced or pressed, or ½ teaspoon garlic powder

Heat in a medium-size skillet or sauté pan over low heat:

> 2 tablespoons olive oil

Cook and stir in the heated oil over low heat until caramelized:

> 1 medium-size onion, chopped

Stir the cooked onion into the potato mixture. Spread into the prepared baking dish and sprinkle with paprika. Bake for 35 minutes, or until browned on top.

Enchiladas

This is a casserole version of enchiladas. If you prefer, the enchiladas may be prepared and heated individually in a microwave or standard oven. Traditionally, enchiladas are served with refried pinto or black beans, Spanish or Mexican rice, and a tossed salad. Adjust the amount of chili powder in the sauce to your taste. This recipe is featured on the cover.

Have ready:

> 1½ pounds firm regular tofu, frozen, thawed, squeezed dry, and torn or chopped into bite-size pieces
>
> 12 corn tortillas or flour tortillas (store-bought or homemade, see page 42)
>
> Chili Gravy or Tomato Sauce (recipes follow)

CHILI GRAVY

Heat in a 3-quart saucepan over low heat:

> 2 tablespoons canola or light olive oil

Cook and stir in the heated oil over low heat until transparent:

> 1 large onion, chopped

Add and cook and stir for a few minutes:

> 3 to 6 tablespoons chili powder
>
> 1 tablespoon ground cumin
>
> 2 cloves garlic, minced or pressed, or 1 teaspoon garlic powder
>
> 1 teaspoon salt

Mix together with a whisk until smooth:

> 1½ quarts water or vegetable broth
>
> 6 tablespoons unbleached flour, or 3 tablespoons cornstarch

Stir or whisk the mixture into the cooked onion, taking care to avoid any lumps. Bring to a boil, reduce the heat, and simmer for 20 minutes.

TOMATO SAUCE

Heat in a 3-quart saucepan over low heat:

> 2 tablespoons canola or olive oil

Cook and stir in the heated oil over low heat:

> 1 large onion, chopped
>
> 3 cloves garlic, minced

When onion is transparent, stir in and heat:

> 2 cans (15 ounces each) tomato sauce

> 2 cups water or vegetable broth
>
> 3 to 6 tablespoons chili powder
>
> 1 tablespoon ground cumin
>
> 1 teaspoon salt

Simmer for 20 minutes.

FOR THE TOFU

While your chosen sauce is simmering, preheat the oven to 350 degrees F, and oil an 11 x 17-inch baking sheet.

Whisk together:

> 3 tablespoons soy sauce
>
> 1 tablespoon natural peanut butter
>
> 2 teaspoons onion powder
>
> 1 teaspoon ground cumin

Pour this mixture over the prepared tofu in a medium-size bowl and squeeze it in evenly (see Freezing Tofu, page 4). Arrange the tofu pieces in a single layer on the prepared baking sheet and bake for 15 minutes.

PUTTING IT ALL TOGETHER

Pour a thin layer of Chili Gravy or Tomato Sauce into a 9 x 13-inch baking pan. Dunk a tortilla in the gravy or sauce in the saucepan, lay it on a plate, then place about ⅓ cup of the tofu filling across the tortilla and roll it up. Repeat this process for all of the tortillas. Arrange the tortillas in the baking pan, seam side down, and cover with the remainder of the sauce.

Sprinkle the top with:

> ¾ cup chopped onion (optional)
>
> ¾ cup chopped black olives (optional)

Bake for 20 to 25 minutes, or until bubbling. Serve with a dollop of Cilantro-Jalapeño Dip (page 15).

Tamale Pie

MAKES 6 TO 8 SERVINGS

This casserole bears no resemblance to Mexican tamales, which it is named after; instead it is a hearty and delicious cornbread-topped pie.

Have ready:

> 1 pound firm regular tofu, frozen, thawed, squeezed dry, and cut or torn into bite-size pieces

Heat in a 3-quart saucepan over low heat:

> 1 tablespoon olive oil

Cook and stir in the heated oil over low heat until crisp-tender:

> 1 large onion, chopped
>
> 1 large bell pepper, chopped
>
> 1 clove garlic, minced

During the last minute of cooking, stir in:

> 2 tablespoons chili powder
>
> 2 teaspoons ground cumin
>
> 1½ teaspoons minced fresh oregano, or ½ teaspoon dried

Stir in the tofu and:

> 1 can (15 ounces) diced tomatoes
>
> 1 can (15 ounces) tomato sauce
>
> 1 package (10 ounces) frozen corn kernels
>
> 1 cup black olives (optional)
>
> 1 can (6 ounces) green chiles, drained and chopped
>
> ¼ cup chopped fresh cilantro

Bring to a boil. Remove from the heat and pour the mixture into a 9 x 13-inch baking pan. Set aside while you prepare the Cornbread Topping (recipe follows). Preheat the oven to 350 degrees F.

FOR THE CORNBREAD TOPPING

Mix together in a bowl:

> 1 cup cornmeal
>
> 1 cup whole wheat pastry flour
>
> 2 teaspoons baking powder
>
> ½ teaspoon salt

Stir together in a separate bowl:

> 1 cup unsweetened soymilk
>
> 2 tablespoons canola or olive oil
>
> 1 tablespoon sweetener of your choice (optional)

Pour into the cornmeal mixture and stir briefly, just to combine. Spoon the mixture over the filling in the baking pan, spreading it out evenly. Bake for about 45 minutes, or until the topping is browned.

70   TOFU COOKERY

Tofu Spinach Pie

This deep-dish pie is another family favorite. I prefer to use fresh spinach, but frozen will do in a pinch.

Have ready:

> 1 (9-inch) pie crust, partially baked
>
> 2 packages (9 ounces each) fresh spinach, coarsely chopped, or 1 package (14 ounces) frozen chopped spinach, thawed and drained

Preheat the oven to 400 degrees F. Heat in a large skillet or sauté pan over low heat:

> 1 tablespoon olive oil

Cook and stir in the heated oil over low heat until caramelized:

> 2 medium-size sweet onions, minced (about 2½ cups)
>
> 3 cloves garlic, minced or pressed

Mix into the caramelized onions and garlic until heated:

> 1 pound firm regular tofu, mashed or crumbled

Stir in the spinach and cook just until wilted. Remove from the heat and mix in:

> 2 tablespoons freshly squeezed lemon juice or apple cider vinegar
>
> 2 tablespoons mellow white miso, or 2 teaspoons salt
>
> ¼ cup nutritional yeast flakes (optional)
>
> ⅛ teaspoon freshly grated nutmeg (optional)

Spoon into the pie crust and bake for about 30 minutes, or until the crust is golden.

Note: When using miso, mix it with the vinegar or lemon juice before adding it to the pie filling for more even distribution.

Chile con Tofu

This is a mild American-style chili with a tomato broth.

Stir together in a bowl:

> 1 pound firm regular tofu, crumbled
>
> 1 tablespoon soy sauce

Heat in a 3-quart soup pot over low heat:

> 2 tablespoons olive or canola oil

Cook and stir in the heated oil over medium heat until the onion is soft:

> 1 medium-size onion, chopped
>
> ½ green bell pepper, chopped

> 1½ tablespoons chili powder
>
> 2 cloves garlic, minced

Stir in the tofu mixture and continue to cook and stir. When the tofu is browned, add to the pot:

> 2½ cups cooked pinto beans, with enough water or vegetable broth to cover
>
> 1 can (16 ounces) tomato sauce
>
> 1 cup water or vegetable broth

Bring to a boil, lower the heat, and simmer until heated through.

Chile con Tofu and Beans

This is a mild Southwestern-style chili made with chewy frozen tofu and a spicy broth. This recipe is pictured on the opposite page.

Have ready:

> 2½ cups cooked pinto beans, with enough water to cover
>
> 1 pound firm to extra-firm regular tofu, frozen, thawed, squeezed dry, and torn into bite-size pieces

Preheat the oven to 350 degrees F, and oil an 11 x 17-inch baking sheet with olive oil. Combine by hand or in a blender:

> ¼ cup water
>
> 2 tablespoons soy sauce
>
> 1 tablespoon natural peanut butter
>
> 1 teaspoon onion powder
>
> ½ teaspoon ground cumin
>
> ¼ teaspoon garlic powder

Pour this mixture over the tofu pieces and press or squeeze it in so all the liquid is absorbed evenly (see Freezing Tofu, page 4). Arrange the tofu pieces on the prepared baking sheet and bake for 20 minutes. Flip the pieces over and bake 10 minutes longer.

Heat in a heavy 2-quart soup pot over low heat:

> 1 tablespoon olive oil

Cook and stir in the heated oil over medium heat until tender:

> 1 large onion, diced
>
> 1 large green bell pepper, diced
>
> 2 cloves garlic, minced

During the last minute of cooking stir in:

> 1 tablespoon chili powder
>
> 1 teaspoon ground cumin

Stir in the beans and water. Then add the baked tofu pieces along with:

> 1 teaspoon salt

Bring to a boil, reduce the heat, and simmer until heated through. Serve hot with Sesame Tofu Crackers (page 143) and your favorite salad.

This is another family favorite and comfort food at its best.

Have ready:

> 1 pound fresh or frozen (thawed and squeezed dry) firm regular tofu, cut into ½-inch cubes
>
> 1 unbaked pie crust (to be used as a top crust), to fit a 2-quart casserole

FOR THE FILLING

Parboil for 10 minutes in water to cover:

> 1 cup cubed potatoes
>
> 1 cup sliced or cubed carrots

Drain the potatoes and carrots and reserve the cooking water. Heat in a large skillet or 2-quart saucepan over medium heat:

> 1 tablespoon olive oil

Cook and stir in the heated oil over low heat:

> 1 medium-size onion, chopped
>
> 1 clove garlic, minced
>
> ½ teaspoon salt

When the onion is soft, add the tofu, potatoes, carrots, and:

> 1 cup fresh or frozen green peas

Cover and set aside while you prepare the gravy. Preheat the oven to 350 degrees F.

FOR THE GRAVY

Let bubble together over low heat for about 1 minute:

> 3 tablespoons canola or light olive oil
>
> 3 tablespoons unbleached flour
>
> 3 tablespoons nutritional yeast flakes

Whisk in:

> 1½ cups reserved vegetable cooking water
>
> 1½ cups unsweetened soymilk
>
> 1 tablespoon minced fresh sage, or 1 teaspoon dried
>
> 1½ teaspoons minced fresh thyme, or ½ teaspoon dried
>
> 1 teaspoon salt
>
> 1 clove garlic, minced or pressed, or ½ teaspoon garlic powder
>
> ½ teaspoon freshly ground black pepper
>
> ½ teaspoon paprika

Heat and stir the gravy with a whisk until it is boiling and thickened with no lumps.

Combine the filling with the gravy in a 2-quart casserole dish. Place and seal the prepared pie crust on top, cutting decorative steam vents in the middle. Bake the pie for 30 to 40 minutes, or until the crust is golden brown and the filling is bubbling.

Onion and Pepper Pie

Here is a unique deep-dish pizza pie with a creamy tofu base and no tomato sauce. Baking it on a pizza stone will create a crispier crust.

FOR THE CRUST

Dissolve in a measuring cup or bowl:

> ½ cup warm water (105 to 115 degrees F)
>
> 1½ teaspoons active dry yeast
>
> 1½ teaspoons sweetener of your choice

Mix together in a food processor or bowl:

> 1½ cups unbleached or whole wheat flour
>
> ¼ teaspoon salt

If using a food processor, pour in the yeast mixture while the machine is running and process until the dough is well kneaded. If mixing by hand, knead the yeast mixture and sweetener into the flour and salt until it forms a smooth ball. Transfer the dough to a lightly oiled bowl, cover, and let rise while you prepare the filling.

Preheat the oven to 450 degrees F. If you have a pizza stone, put it in the oven to heat while the oven is preheating.

FOR THE FILLING

Heat in a large skillet or sauté pan over low heat:

> 1 tablespoon olive oil

Cook and stir in the heated oil over medium heat until crisp-tender:

> 2 medium-size onions, thinly sliced
>
> 1 medium-size green bell pepper, thinly sliced

> 1 medium-size red bell pepper, thinly sliced
>
> 1 clove garlic, minced

Process in a food processor or blender until smooth and creamy:

> 1 pound medium-firm regular tofu, mashed or crumbled
>
> 1 tablespoon olive oil
>
> 1½ teaspoons minced fresh basil, or ½ teaspoon dried
>
> 1½ teaspoons minced fresh oregano, or ½ teaspoon dried
>
> ½ teaspoon salt
>
> 1 clove garlic, minced or pressed, or ½ teaspoon garlic powder

PUTTING IT ALL TOGETHER

Roll the dough out on a board sprinkled with cornmeal to fit a 12-inch pizza pan or preheated pizza stone. Spread the tofu filling evenly over the dough. Then distribute the onion and peppers evenly over the top. Bake the pie for 10 to 15 minutes, or until the crust is golden.

Layered Casserole

This dish is especially attractive when made in a glass soufflé dish. Layered Casserole is pictured on the opposite page.

Oil a 3-quart glass soufflé or casserole dish with:

> 1 tablespoon olive oil

Dust the baking dish with:

> 2 tablespoons unbleached flour

Process each layer separately in a food processor or blender, and spread it evenly into the baking dish. Be careful not to mix the layers.

FOR THE FIRST LAYER

> 3 cups chopped fresh spinach, cooked and drained, or 1 package (10 ounces) frozen chopped spinach, cooked and drained
>
> 1 pound medium-firm regular tofu, crumbled
>
> 1 teaspoon salt

FOR THE SECOND LAYER

> 1 pound medium-firm regular tofu, crumbled
>
> 1 jar (7 ounces) pimientos, drained
>
> 1 tablespoon freshly squeezed lemon juice
>
> 1 teaspoon salt

FOR THE THIRD LAYER

> 1½ pounds medium-firm regular tofu, crumbled
>
> 2 tablespoons soy sauce
>
> 1 tablespoon minced onion, or 1 teaspoon onion powder
>
> 1 clove garlic, minced or pressed, or ½ teaspoon garlic powder
>
> 1 teaspoon salt

Fold into the third-layer mixture:

> 1 cup finely chopped mushrooms

Preheat the oven to 350 degrees F. Bake the casserole for 1 hour, or until it is set and little cracks start to form on top. Let stand and cool for a few minutes before serving. Serve hot or cold.

Zucchini Frittata

This tasty dish makes a colorful and impressive presentation at any meal. Using ground flaxseeds rather than flour to bind this frittata will result in a slightly lighter consistency.

Heat in a large skillet or sauté pan over low heat:

>   1 tablespoon olive oil

Cook and stir in the heated oil over medium heat until crisp-tender:

>   4 medium-size zucchini, thinly sliced
>
>   1 large onion, thinly sliced
>
>   ¼ cup chopped fresh parsley
>
>   3 tablespoons chopped fresh basil
>
>   3 cloves garlic, pressed

Remove from the heat. Stir together in a large bowl:

>   ¾ pound firm regular tofu, processed in a food processor or blender until smooth
>
>   ¼ pound firm regular tofu, mashed or crumbled (½ cup)
>
>   3 tablespoons ground flaxseeds, or ¾ cup unbleached flour
>
>   1 tablespoon soy sauce
>
>   2 teaspoons baking powder
>
>   1½ teaspoons salt

Fold in the cooked vegetables. Preheat the oven to 350 degrees F, and oil an 11 x 17-inch baking sheet.

For each frittata, scoop out ½ cup of the tofu mixture and place it on the prepared baking sheet. Spread each scoop into a 5-inch circle; the mixture should make about 8 frittatas. Bake the frittatas for 15 minutes on one side, then gently flip them over and bake 15 minutes longer, or until golden brown. Let the frittatas cool for a few minutes to set before removing them from the baking sheet. Serve with wide semolina or whole grain noodles and Tomato Sauce Topping (recipe follows).

VARIATION

For one large frittata, heat a 10-inch cast-iron skillet in the oven, oil the hot skillet, and spread the mixture evenly inside. Bake for about 30 minutes, or until browned on top.

TOMATO SAUCE TOPPING

Makes 2 cups

Stir together in a 2-quart saucepan over low heat:

>   1 can (15 ounces) tomato sauce
>
>   ¼ cup water
>
>   3 tablespoons minced fresh Italian parsley
>
>   2 teaspoons wine vinegar
>
>   ½ teaspoon garlic powder
>
>   ½ teaspoon salt

Simmer for 20 minutes. Pour over the hot frittatas.

Tofu Rancheros

This is an adaptation of a classic Mexican dish that is traditionally made with eggs and served for breakfast with refried pinto beans and sweet coffee. The term rancheros refers to a rustic style of cooking that is done outdoors. Ranchero sauce derives its name from being cooked rapidly in a frying pan over an open fire.

Prepare and set aside:

> 3 large or 4 medium-size ripe tomatoes, cut into wedges
>
> 1 large onion, chopped
>
> ¼ cup chopped fresh cilantro or parsley
>
> 2 cloves garlic, chopped

Cut into 8 slices and sprinkle with a little salt:

> 1 pound soft to medium-firm regular tofu

Heat a dry heavy skillet over medium-high heat. When the skillet is hot, place one at a time on the hot surface so they puff up quickly on each side:

> 8 corn tortillas

The tortillas should be heated but soft. Wrap the heated tortillas in a towel to keep them warm until the tofu is cooked.

In the same hot skillet, quickly brown the tofu slices on each side in:

> 1 tablespoon light olive or canola oil

Remove the tofu from the skillet and set aside. Immediately add the chopped onion and garlic to the hot skillet and cook and stir until they start to brown.

Add the tomato wedges to the skillet, stir, cover, and steam for 3 minutes.

Stir in, cover, and steam for 3 minutes:

> 1 can (6 ounces) chopped green chiles
>
> 1 teaspoon salt
>
> Dash of ground cumin

Put 2 hot tortillas on each plate, side by side. Put 1 slice of the browned tofu on each tortilla. When the tomatoes are soft and saucy, but before they lose their shape completely, remove from the heat and pour the vegetables equally over the tortillas and tofu. Serve immediately, garnished with the chopped cilantro or parsley.

Stewart's Stew

This hearty stew is another family comfort-food favorite.

Place in a glass or stainless steel pan:

> 1½ pounds firm to extra-firm regular tofu, cut into ¾-inch cubes

Pour over the tofu:

> ½ cup soy sauce

Let the tofu marinate in the refrigerator while you prepare the vegetables.

Combine in a 5-quart saucepan and boil until the vegetables are almost soft:

> 2½ quarts water
>
> 6 carrots, cut into ¾-inch cubes
>
> 5 medium-size potatoes, cut into ¾-inch cubes
>
> 4 medium-size onions, coarsely chopped
>
> ½ teaspoon salt

Drain the soy sauce from the tofu and pour it into the vegetables.

Combine in a paper or plastic bag:

> 1 cup whole wheat pastry or unbleached flour
>
> 1 teaspoon salt
>
> 1 teaspoon freshly ground black pepper

Close the bag tightly and shake it to combine the ingredients. Add the drained tofu cubes, close the bag tightly, and shake again to coat them.

Heat in a large skillet or sauté pan over low heat:

> 2 to 4 tablespoons canola or light olive oil

Brown the tofu cubes on all sides in the heated oil over medium heat. Be careful not to knock off the breading when turning the cubes. Add the tofu to the almost-soft vegetables. Mix any left-over breading into a smooth paste with a little of the broth, then add to the stew. Simmer until heated through.

Stir-Fries

Tofu is not just for stir-fries, but it does work very well in them. Stir-fries originated in Asia as an economical cooking method that is also very tasty. It is an excellent way to prepare crisp-tender vegetables, since everything is cooked quickly over relatively high heat. A wok is the optimum tool for stir-frying, but it is not essential. A large skillet or sauté pan will suffice for this kind of cooking. It is crucial to have the pan and oil hot but not smoking before adding the ingredients.

Almond Tofu, page 82

Almond Tofu

Crisp vegetables, crunchy almonds, and soft tofu make an interesting, satisfying, and colorful combination. Almond Tofu is pictured on page 81.

FOR THE TOFU

Whisk together in a large bowl:

¼ cup soy sauce

1 tablespoon almond butter or natural peanut butter

1 teaspoon onion powder

1 clove garlic, minced or pressed, or ½ teaspoon garlic powder

Add and mix in gently:

2 pounds firm regular tofu, cut into ¾-inch cubes

Heat in a skillet or sauté pan over medium heat:

1 to 2 tablespoons olive oil

Add the tofu mixture and cook over medium heat until the liquid is absorbed and the tofu is browned.

FOR THE VEGETABLES

Heat in a wok, large skillet, or sauté pan over medium-high heat:

1 tablespoon olive oil

Cook and stir in the heated oil over medium-high heat until crisp-tender:

1 large bell pepper, cut into 1-inch squares

6 to 8 green onions, cut into 1½-inch pieces

3 stalks celery, cut into 1-inch pieces

1 can (8 ounces) sliced water chestnuts, drained

1 tablespoon grated fresh ginger, or 1 teaspoon ground ginger

FOR THE SAUCE

While the vegetables are cooking, shake together in a jar or blend in a blender:

2 cups cold water

¼ cup soy sauce

2 tablespoons cornstarch

When the vegetables are crisp-tender, pour the cornstarch mixture over them and simmer and stir until the sauce is thickened. Stir in the browned tofu and:

½ cup roasted almonds

Serve hot over hot brown rice or pasta.

VARIATION

Cashew Tofu: Replace the almonds with ½ cup raw or roasted cashews.

Walnut Broccoli Stir-Fry

Brightly colored broccoli and carrots team up with tofu, onions, mushrooms, and walnuts for a healthful, quick, and easy stir-fry.

Heat in a medium-size skillet or sauté pan over medium heat:

> 1 tablespoon olive oil

Add to the heated oil and brown lightly:

> 1 pound firm regular tofu, cut into 1-inch cubes

In a 2-quart saucepan, bring to a boil:

> 1 cup water
> ½ teaspoon salt

Drop into the boiling salted water and boil for 1 minute:

> 2 cups broccoli florets, with 1- to 2-inch stems
> 2 carrots, thinly sliced

Drain and set aside the cooking liquid. When it is cool, stir in:

> 3 tablespoons soy sauce
> 1 tablespoon cornstarch
> ½ teaspoon freshly ground black pepper

Heat in a wok, large skillet, or sauté pan over medium heat:

> 1 tablespoon olive oil

Cook and stir in the heated oil over medium heat until soft:

> 2 onions, thinly sliced

Add and continue to cook and stir for 2 minutes:

> 1 cup sliced mushrooms
> ½ cup walnut halves

Increase the heat to medium-high and add the parboiled carrots and broccoli. Cook and stir for 1 minute, then add the browned tofu cubes and cook and stir for 1 minute longer.

Pour the seasoned cooking liquid over the hot vegetables and tofu, and cook and stir until bubbling. Serve hot over rice or Chinese noodles.

VARIATION

Replace the broccoli with broccoli rabe.

Stir-Fried Chinese Cabbage and Tofu

Chinese, or napa, cabbage is commonly found in grocery stores. There are many different varieties of Asian greens that could also be used for this stir-fry.

Have ready:

> 1 pound firm to extra-firm regular tofu, cut into 1 x ½ x ¼-inch pieces
>
> 1 piece (1-inch cube) peeled fresh ginger, sliced
>
> 2 cloves garlic, crushed with the side of a knife or cleaver
>
> ¼ teaspoon vegetarian bouillon powder dissolved in 2 tablespoons water
>
> 1½ teaspoons cornstarch mixed with 2 tablespoons cold water
>
> 4 cups chopped Chinese cabbage, cut into 1-inch pieces (keep the crunchy stem and leafy parts separate)

Heat in a wok, large skillet, or sauté pan over low heat:

> 1 tablespoon canola oil

Add the ginger and half of the crushed garlic to the heated oil and fry until brown. Remove the ginger and garlic from the wok and discard.

Immediately add the tofu pieces to the flavored oil in the wok and gently stir to coat them.

Sprinkle over the coated tofu:

> 1 tablespoon soy sauce
>
> ¼ teaspoon salt

Cook and stir gently for 2 minutes. Transfer the tofu and all of the liquid in the wok to a bowl.

In the same wok, heat:

> 1 tablespoon canola oil

Add the remaining garlic and cook and stir until brown. Remove the garlic and discard. Immediately add the stem sections of the Chinese cabbage and cook and stir for 1 minute. Then add the dissolved bouillon and:

> ¼ teaspoon salt

Cover and steam for 2 minutes. Add the leafy sections of the Chinese cabbage and cook and stir for 1 minute. Cover and cook for 1 minute longer.

Return the tofu and liquid to the pan. Stir the cornstarch mixture, drizzle it into the center of the wok where the liquid has collected, and cook and stir until thickened. Serve immediately.

Tofu and Broccoli in Garlic Sauce

This tasty garlic sauce adds special zip to tofu and broccoli. For a change, try broccoli rabe in place of the broccoli.

FOR THE TOFU

Place in a 9 x 13-inch glass or stainless steel pan:

> 1½ pounds firm regular tofu, cut into ½-inch cubes

Pour evenly over the tofu cubes:

> ¼ cup soy sauce

Cover and marinate in the refrigerator, carefully stirring and turning the tofu over occasionally while you prepare the sauce.

FOR THE VEGETABLES AND SAUCE

Have ready in separate bowls:

> 2 medium-size onions, cut in half lengthwise and thinly sliced
>
> 8 ounces mushrooms, sliced
>
> 8 to 10 cloves garlic, crushed
>
> 1 pound broccoli, cut into large florets

Dissolve together and set aside:

> 2 cups boiling water
>
> 2 cubes vegetable bouillon

PUTTING IT ALL TOGETHER:

Drain the tofu and reserve the liquid. Heat in a large heavy skillet or wok over medium heat:

> 2 tablespoon olive or canola oil

Brown the marinated tofu on all sides in the heated oil over medium heat. Remove the tofu and set it aside. Add to the hot pan:

> 1 tablespoon olive or canola oil

Add the onions and mushrooms and cook and stir them over medium heat until they start to soften. Stir in the crushed garlic, bouillon mixture, and:

> 3 tablespoons sweetener of your choice
>
> 1 tablespoon prepared Chinese hot mustard
>
> 1 teaspoon crushed red pepper flakes
>
> 1 teaspoon grated fresh ginger, or ¼ teaspoon ground ginger

Stir in the tofu and reserved liquid and simmer over medium heat for 1 minute. Stir in the broccoli and simmer for 3 minutes longer. Cover, remove from the heat, and let stand for 5 minutes. Serve over your favorite rice, whole grain, or pasta.

Fresh Shiitake Stir-Fry

The shiitake is a forest mushroom from Asia that grows on hardwood logs. It is a healthful food containing all eight amino acids in good proportion. Look for shiitakes in natural food stores, Asian groceries, and specialty produce shops. Fresh Shiitake Stir-Fry is pictured on the opposite page.

Place in a small glass or stainless steel pan or bowl:

> 1 pound firm to extra-firm regular tofu, cut into ½-inch cubes

To make the marinade, chop together in a food processor:

> 1 piece (1-inch cube) peeled fresh ginger
>
> 2 cloves garlic

Add to the food processor and blend:

> ¼ cup mirin
>
> 2 tablespoons soy sauce

Pour this mixture over the tofu cubes, cover, and place in the refrigerator to marinate while you prepare the vegetables.

Place in separate bowls:

> 1 red bell pepper, cut into triangles
>
> ½ cup sliced green onions
>
> ½ pound snow peas, washed and stems removed
>
> 3½ ounces fresh shiitake mushrooms, sliced

Heat in a wok, large skillet, or sauté pan over low heat:

> 1 tablespoon olive oil

Add the bell pepper and green onions to the heated oil and cook and stir over medium-high heat for 1 minute. Add the snow peas and mushrooms and cook and stir for 1 minute. Add the tofu and marinade and cook and stir for 1 minute. Cover and steam until the tofu and vegetables are hot. Serve over brown rice or pasta.

Note: If fresh shiitake mushrooms are not available, dried ones can be reconstituted in water. One ounce of dried shiitake mushrooms is equal to about ½ pound fresh, so for this recipe, use about ½ ounce dried mushrooms. Rinse the dried shiitakes well and discard the water. Fill a bowl or pot with fresh water, add the dried mushrooms, cover them with a plate or pot lid to keep them under the water, and let the mushrooms soak for about 6 hours. Drain and reserve the water for stock. Wipe off any dirt on the caps or gills.

Burgers, Patties, Balls, and Filled Rolls

One of our favorite comfort foods, the burger, has gone meatless. Although there are many similar meatless products available commercially, making your own gives you the ultimate choice of what goes into them. Homemade burgers, and their cousins, patties and balls, provide an ideal venue to add more vegetables, nuts, and whole grains to your diet. The addition of ground flaxseeds to many of these recipes makes for a more substantial binding of the somewhat fragile mixtures used for these popular foods.

Tofu Spaghetti Balls

Tofu Spaghetti Balls

Top your next spaghetti dinner with these tasty tofu balls, pictured on the opposite page.

Preheat the oven to 350 degrees F, and oil an 8-inch square baking pan.

Mix together:

> 1 pound firm regular tofu, mashed
>
> ½ cup wheat germ, or 2 tablespoons ground flaxseeds
>
> ¼ cup chopped fresh parsley
>
> 2 tablespoons soy sauce
>
> 2 tablespoons nutritional yeast flakes (optional)
>
> ¼ cup chopped onion, or 1 tablespoon onion powder
>
> 1 teaspoon minced fresh oregano, or ¼ teaspoon dried
>
> 1 clove garlic, minced or pressed, or ½ teaspoon garlic powder
>
> ¼ teaspoon freshly ground black pepper

If you use ground flaxseeds, let the mixture sit for about 30 minutes to make it easier to work with. Use about 2 tablespoons of the mixture to form each 1½-inch ball, for a total of 16 balls. Arrange the balls equidistant in the prepared baking pan. Bake for about 30 minutes, turning them carefully (they will be delicate) about every 10 minutes to maintain a round shape, until they are browned. Let the balls cool for a few minutes to set before serving.

Sloppy Joes

This is a classic American dish, but instead of ground beef it is made with tofu, which soaks up the flavors beautifully. Frozen tofu will create a chewier version.

Heat in a large skillet or sauté pan over low heat:

> 2 tablespoons olive oil

Cook and stir in the heated oil over low heat until tender:

> 1 medium-size onion, chopped
>
> 1 medium-size green bell pepper, chopped
>
> 2 cloves garlic, minced

Stir in:

> 1 pound fresh or frozen (thawed and squeezed dry) firm regular tofu, crumbled
>
> 2 tablespoons soy sauce

Continue cooking and stirring until the tofu starts to brown. Stir in:

> 2 cups tomato sauce (your favorite or Basic Italian-Style Tomato Sauce, page 108)
>
> 1 tablespoon chili powder
>
> ½ teaspoon ground cumin

Simmer until bubbling. Serve hot over split and toasted whole grain burger buns.

These are the original seaside cakes based on New England crab cakes. They are pictured below.

To make a white sauce, combine in a medium-size skillet or sauté pan:

> ¼ cup olive oil
>
> ¼ cup unbleached flour

Let bubble over medium heat for 1 to 2 minutes. Taking care to avoid any lumps, slowly whisk in:

> 1 cup unsweetened soymilk
>
> ½ teaspoon salt

Stir in and continue cooking until the sauce is very thick:

> 2 tablespoons minced onion

Combine in a bowl:

> 1 pound firm regular tofu, crumbled
>
> 1 teaspoon salt
>
> ½ teaspoon dry mustard
>
> Dash of cayenne

Stir the white sauce into the tofu mixture. Cover and chill in the refrigerator for 3 to 4 hours.

Shape the chilled mixture into cakes, 1½ inches round by ½ inch thick. Roll the cakes in a mixture of:

> 12 to 16 soda crackers, crushed into crumbs
>
> 1½ teaspoons paprika

Chill the crumb-covered cakes for about 1 hour. (At this point the cakes can be frozen for later use.)

Heat in a large skillet or sauté pan over medium heat:

> 2 to 3 tablespoons olive oil

Brown the prepared cakes on both sides in the heated oil, turning them gently. Serve with lemon wedges, Tartar Sauce (page 50), or cocktail sauce, and garnish with fresh parsley or watercress.

Seaside Cakes

Quick Seaside Cakes

With the flavor of the sea, these quick and easy savory cakes are sure to please. The ingredients are bound together by ground flax or chia seeds. Chia seeds are a high-protein superfood, rich in the essential fatty acids omega-3 and omega-6. Chia was historically used as a protein source by the original peoples of Mexico.

Whisk together in a medium-size bowl and let stand until thickened (about 30 minutes for flaxseeds and 10 minutes for chia seeds):

> ½ cup unsweetened soymilk
>
> 1½ tablespoons ground flaxseeds, or 1 tablespoon ground chia seeds

Heat in a small skillet or sauté pan over low heat:

> 1½ teaspoons olive oil

Cook and stir in the heated oil over low heat until crisp-tender:

> 2 tablespoons minced onion
>
> 2 tablespoons minced red bell pepper
>
> 2 tablespoons minced celery

Stir the hot cooked vegetables into the soymilk mixture along with:

> 1 teaspoon kelp powder, or 1 tablespoon nori or dulse flakes
>
> ½ teaspoon salt
>
> ½ teaspoon paprika
>
> ¼ teaspoon dry mustard
>
> Dash of cayenne, or ⅛ teaspoon crushed red pepper flakes

Add and mix in well:

> ½ pound firm regular tofu, crumbled

Have ready:

> 14 to 16 whole wheat soda crackers, crushed

To make each cake, drop 2 tablespoons of the tofu mixture into the cracker crumbs and form it into a ¼-inch-thick patty, making sure it is coated all over with the crumbs. Continue in this fashion until all of the tofu mixture is used. This will make 12 to 14 cakes.

Heat in a large skillet over medium heat:

> 1 tablespoon olive oil

Brown the cakes in the oil on both sides, adding more oil as needed for the second side. Let the cakes cool slightly to set before serving. Serve with lemon wedges, Tartar Sauce (page 50), or cocktail sauce. Garnish with fresh parsley, arugula, or watercress.

Chinese Sweet-and-Sour Balls

This delicious and attractive dish is pictured on the opposite page.

Preheat the oven to 350 degrees F, and oil an 8-inch square baking pan with canola or light olive oil.

Whisk together in a small bowl:

> 1 tablespoon natural peanut butter
>
> 1 tablespoon soy sauce

Place in a large bowl and mash:

> 1 pound firm regular tofu

Stir the peanut butter mixture into the tofu along with:

> ½ cup unbleached flour, or 2 tablespoons ground flaxseeds
>
> ½ cup finely chopped green bell pepper
>
> 4 green onions, thinly sliced
>
> ¼ cup sliced mushrooms
>
> ¼ cup sliced water chestnuts or celery

Form into 16 balls, each about 1½ inches in diameter, and arrange them in the prepared baking pan.

Bake for 20 minutes, then carefully turn each ball over and bake for 20 minutes longer. Let the balls cool for a few minutes to set before removing them from the pan. Serve on rice, and top with Sweet-and-Sour Sauce (recipe follows).

SWEET-AND SOUR-SAUCE

Combine in a saucepan over medium heat:

> 1 cup unsweetened pineapple juice
>
> 6 tablespoons sweetener of your choice
>
> 6 tablespoons apple cider vinegar
>
> 2 tablespoons soy sauce
>
> 1½ tablespoons arrowroot or cornstarch
>
> 1 clove garlic, minced or pressed, or ½ teaspoon garlic powder

Cook over medium-low heat for about 20 minutes, or until thickened, whisking to avoid lumps.

Tofu Burgers

Serve this basic burger on a bun with all the fixings.

Mix and mash together in a bowl:

> 1 pound firm regular tofu, crumbled
>
> ¼ cup wheat germ
>
> ¼ cup whole wheat flour
>
> 2 tablespoons nutritional yeast flakes
>
> 1 tablespoon grated onion
>
> ½ teaspoon garlic powder
>
> ½ teaspoon poultry seasoning
>
> ¼ teaspoon freshly ground black pepper

Form into 6 burgers, each 3 inches in diameter. Heat in a large skillet over medium heat:

> 1 tablespoon olive oil

Brown the burgers on each side in the heated oil over medium heat, adding more oil as necessary.

Mushroom Tofu Burgers

These savory burgers will have a subtle change of flavor depending on what type of mushroom is used. Frozen tofu gives them a chewy texture.

Heat in a medium-size skillet or sauté pan over low heat:

> 1 tablespoon olive oil

Cook and stir in the heated oil over medium heat until the onion is soft:

> 8 ounces mushrooms of your choice, chopped (about 3 cups)
>
> ½ cup chopped green bell pepper
>
> ½ cup chopped onion
>
> ¼ cup chopped fresh parsley
>
> 1 teaspoon dried savory
>
> 1 clove garlic, minced

Mix together in a bowl:

> 1 pound firm regular tofu, frozen, thawed, squeezed dry, and crumbled

> 2 tablespoons ground flaxseeds
>
> 2 tablespoons soy sauce
>
> ¼ teaspoon freshly ground black pepper

Stir the cooked vegetable mixture into the tofu mixture. Let stand for at least 30 minutes to allow the flaxseeds to bind the ingredients.

Preheat the oven to 350 degrees F, and oil a 9 x 13-inch baking sheet. Form the mixture into 6 to 8 burgers, place them on the prepared baking sheet, and bake for about 15 minutes on each side. Alternatively, heat a little olive oil in a large skillet or sauté pan and brown the burgers on both sides. Let the burgers cool for a few minutes to set before serving.

Walnut Tofu Beet Burgers

Frozen tofu gives these flavorful burgers a chewy texture and beets give a rich color.

Mix together:

> ½ cup chopped onion
>
> 1 clove garlic, pressed
>
> 1 cup finely grated raw beets
>
> 6 tablespoons finely chopped walnuts (about 1½ ounces)
>
> 2 tablespoons soy sauce
>
> 2 tablespoons balsamic vinegar
>
> 1 pound firm regular tofu, frozen, thawed, squeezed dry, and crumbled
>
> ¼ cup chopped fresh parsley

> 2 tablespoons ground flax seed
>
> 1 tablespoon olive oil

Let the burger mixture stand for at least thirty minutes allowing the flax to develop to bind the burgers together. Preheat the oven to 350 degrees F. Form the mixture into 6 to 8 burgers, place them on an oiled 9 x 13-inch baking sheet and bake for about 15 minutes on each side. Alternatively, heat a little olive oil in a large skillet or sauté pan and brown the burgers on both sides. Let the burgers cool for a few minutes to set before serving.

Tofu Mushroom Roll

This comfort-food favorite is served often at our house, especially for mushroom lovers.

FOR THE FILLING

Heat in a medium-size skillet or sauté pan over low heat:

> 1 tablespoon canola or olive oil

Cook and stir in the heated oil over low heat:

> 8 ounces mushrooms, chopped

Heat in another medium-size skillet or sauté pan over low heat:

> 1 tablespoon canola or olive oil

Cook and stir in the heated oil over low heat until transparent:

> ¾ cup chopped onions

Stir together in a large bowl:

> 1½ pounds firm regular tofu, crumbled
> ⅓ cup chopped fresh parley
> 1 teaspoon salt
> ¾ teaspoon ground thyme
> ¼ teaspoon freshly ground black pepper

Set aside one-third of the cooked onions for the sauce. Stir in the remaining cooked onions and all of the cooked mushrooms.

FOR THE DOUGH

Mix together in a large bowl:

> 3 cups unbleached or whole wheat pastry flour
> 4½ teaspoons baking powder
> 1 teaspoon salt

Stir in:

> ½ cup canola or olive oil

Stir in:

> 1 scant cup cold water

Mix well to form a ball. Roll out on a well-floured board into an oblong shape, about ½ inch thick.

PUTTING IT ALL TOGETHER

Preheat the oven to 400 degrees F, and oil an 11 x 17-inch baking sheet. Spread the filling evenly over the rolled-out dough, being careful not to tear the dough. Leave a 1-inch border on one lengthwise edge. Roll up the dough lengthwise and seal the edge with water. Place the roll on the prepared baking sheet and cut a few diagonal slits on the top with a sharp knife. Brush the roll lightly with olive oil and bake for 25 to 30 minutes, or until lightly browned.

FOR THE SAUCE

Heat in a medium-size skillet or sauté pan over low heat:

> 1 tablespoon canola or light olive oil

Cook and stir in the heated oil over low heat until soft:

> 8 ounces mushrooms, sliced

Set the mushrooms aside. Heat in a large skillet or sauté pan over low heat and let bubble together for 1 minute:

> ½ cup unbleached flour
> 2 tablespoons canola or olive oil

Stir in:

> 4 cups vegetable broth or unsweetened soymilk
> 1 tablespoon soy sauce
> ¼ teaspoon freshly ground black pepper

Cook and stir the sauce until thickened, being careful to avoid any lumps. The sauce will be thin. Stir in the cooked mushrooms and reserved onions.

Serve slices of the roll topped with some of the sauce.

This is an egg-free version of egg foo yong. It is pictured on the opposite page.

Heat in a large skillet or wok over medium heat:

> 2 tablespoons canola oil

Cook and stir in the heated oil over low heat for about 5 minutes:

> 1 cup sliced snow peas, cut into 1-inch pieces
>
> 1 cup sliced mushrooms
>
> 8 green onions, cut into 1½-inch pieces (green and white parts)
>
> 1 can (8 ounces) sliced water chestnuts

When the vegetables are crisp-tender, remove from the heat and mix in:

> 2 cups fresh bean sprouts

Preheat the oven to 325 degrees F, and oil an 11 x 17-inch baking sheet. Process in a blender or food processor until smooth and creamy:

> 1¾ pounds soft regular tofu, mashed or crumbled
>
> 2 tablespoons soy sauce

Pour the mixture into a large bowl and mix well with:

> ¾ cup unbleached flour
>
> ¼ pound soft regular tofu, mashed or crumbled (½ cup)
>
> 3 tablespoons nutritional yeast flakes (optional)
>
> 2 teaspoons baking powder

Fold in the cooked vegetables. On the prepared baking sheet, form the mixture into 6 to 8 rounds, each about 5 inches in diameter and ½ inch thick, using about ½ cup of the mixture for each round. Leave about 1 inch of space between the rounds. Bake for 30 minutes, gently flip the rounds over, and bake for 15 minutes longer. Let the rounds cool for a few minutes on the baking sheet. Serve hot over rice or noodles with Mushroom Gravy (recipe follows).

MUSHROOM GRAVY

Mix together in a 2-quart saucepan:

> 2 cups cold water
>
> ½ cup diced mushrooms
>
> ¼ cup soy sauce
>
> 2 tablespoons cornstarch

Cook and stir over low heat for about 20 minutes, or until thickened.

Falafel

Baking rather than frying these falafel significantly lowers the fat content. If you don't have time to cook dried beans, use canned instead. If you are using a blender instead of a food processor, process only one cup of the beans at a time. Falafel is pictured on the opposite page.

FOR THE FALAFEL

Preheat the oven to 350 degrees F, and oil an 11 x 17-inch baking sheet. Process in a food processor or blender until smooth and creamy:

> 4 cups cooked chickpeas, or 2 cans (16 ounces each) chickpeas, drained
>
> 1 cup cooking liquid or water
>
> 3 cloves garlic

Pour the bean mixture into a large bowl and stir in:

> 6 cups fresh whole grain bread crumbs
>
> 1 pound firm regular tofu, mashed
>
> 1 medium-size onion, minced
>
> 1/3 cup soy sauce
>
> 1 teaspoon salt (optional)
>
> 1/4 teaspoon freshly ground black pepper

Mix until all of the ingredients are evenly distributed and moist. Form into 1½-inch balls using about 3 tablespoons of the mixture for each ball. Place the balls equidistant on the prepared baking sheet. Bake for about 30 minutes, carefully turning the balls every 10 minutes to brown them evenly.

Note: Alternatively, the falafel may be deep-fried. Roll the balls in unbleached flour and brown them in a heavy skillet in ½ inch of olive or canola oil heated to 365 to 368 degrees F, gently turning each one until golden all over.

PUTTING IT ALL TOGETHER

Cut 8 to 10 pita breads in half and open the pockets carefully. If you like, the pita breads may be warmed beforehand. To warm them, preheat the oven to 350 degrees F. Wrap 4 or 5 breads together in foil and place them in the oven for about 15 minutes; they should be warm but remain soft. Put 2 to 3 balls in each pita pocket, depending on the size of the bread. Pour about 1 tablespoon of Tahini Sauce (recipe follows) or Tahini Tofu Lemon Sauce (page 46) over the falafel in the pita pocket, and top with chopped tomatoes, cucumber, and lettuce.

TAHINI SAUCE

Mince in a food processor or blender:

> 3 cloves garlic

Add and process until smooth:

> ½ cup tahini
>
> ¼ cup freshly squeezed lemon juice
>
> 2 tablespoons soy sauce

The sauce may be gently warmed or served cold. It will keep for up to 2 weeks in the refrigerator. Tahini Sauce is also delicious on salads, steamed vegetables, fried tofu, and noodles.

This is an old family recipe updated with tofu.

Have ready:

> 1 cup cooked brown or white rice

FOR THE SAUCE

Mix in a large saucepan:

> 7 cups water
>
> 1 can (6 ounces) tomato paste
>
> 6 tablespoons sweetener of your choice
>
> ¼ cup raisins
>
> 2 tablespoons freshly squeezed lemon juice
>
> 1½ teaspoons salt

Let simmer while you prepare the filling.

FOR THE FILLING

Heat in a large skillet or sauté pan over medium heat:

> 2 tablespoons olive oil

Cook and stir in the heated oil over low heat until limp:

> 1 medium-size onion, chopped
>
> 1 clove garlic, minced

Remove from the heat and mix in the cooked rice and:

> 1½ pounds firm regular tofu, mashed
>
> 2 tablespoons soy sauce
>
> 1 teaspoon salt

PUTTING IT ALL TOGETHER

Wash 18 large cabbage leaves. Cook 3 or 4 leaves at a time in boiling water for 1 to 2 minutes to soften. Drain and trim out the hard center core. Put 2 to 3 tablespoons of the filling on each leaf, fold the sides in, and roll up. Use toothpicks to hold the rolls together, if necessary.

Carefully drop the rolls into the simmering sauce without stirring (so they don't fall apart). Simmer for 2 to 3 hours without stirring; push down on the top rolls occasionally and carefully turn them over so they cook evenly. Take the toothpicks out before serving. Serve the cabbage rolls over mashed potatoes or rice.

Pasta with Tofu

Pasta is a natural with tofu. Transforming tofu into a superb, creamy, ricotta-like filling for Italian pasta dishes is one of the best ways to introduce it to skeptics. Because tofu absorbs whatever flavorful sauce is added to it, you will find it particularly well suited to these dishes. Look for pasta made from whole wheat flour for a more healthful choice. For those who are sensitive to wheat or gluten, wheat-free pasta is available at natural food stores and well-stocked supermarkets; it is usually made from rice, potatoes, corn, mung beans, soy, or other gluten-free ingredients.

Pasta Primavera, page 102

Enjoy this refreshing combination of spring vegetables with your favorite pasta. This recipe is pictured on page 101.

FOR THE TOFU AND VEGETABLES

Cut into 2 x ½ x ⅛-inch pieces:

> 1 pound firm regular tofu

Marinate the tofu covered in the refrigerator for at least 2 hours in a mixture of:

> 2 tablespoons soy sauce
>
> 2 tablespoons wine vinegar

Drain the tofu and reserve the marinade. Brown the tofu lightly in:

> 1 tablespoon olive oil

Pour the leftover marinade over the tofu while browning the second side and let it evaporate. Set the tofu aside.

Cook in 1 inch of boiling water until almost tender:

> 4 cups fresh or frozen broccoli florets
>
> 1½ cups fresh or frozen peas

Drain and reserve the cooking water. Heat in a small skillet or sauté pan over low heat:

> 1 tablespoon olive oil

Cook and stir in the heated oil until soft:

> 1 cup sliced mushrooms

FOR THE PASTA

Cook in boiling water until tender:

> 1 pound semolina or whole wheat spaghetti, vermicelli, or your favorite pasta

Drain in a colander and set aside.

FOR THE SAUCE

Let bubble together gently for 3 minutes over low heat:

> ⅓ cup olive oil
>
> ⅓ cup unbleached flour

Whisk in, being careful to avoid lumps:

> 3 cups reserved cooking water (plus additional water as needed to equal 3 cups) or unsweetened soymilk

Stir in:

> ½ cup chopped fresh parsley
>
> 1½ teaspoons salt
>
> ½ teaspoon garlic powder
>
> ⅛ teaspoon cayenne

Cook and stir the sauce over low heat until it is thickened and smooth. Stir in the tofu, broccoli, peas, and mushrooms. Serve hot over the spaghetti.

VARIATION

Broccoli-Asparagus Pasta Primavera: Replace 2 cups of the broccoli florets with 2 cups sliced asparagus, cut into 1-inch pieces.

Curried Cashew Tofu over Pasta

FOR THE TOFU AND PASTA

Cut into 1 x ½ x ¼-inch pieces and place in a bowl:

> 1 pound firm or extra-firm regular tofu, frozen, thawed, and squeezed dry

Mix by hand or process together in a blender:

> ¼ cup water
>
> 2 tablespoons soy sauce
>
> 1 tablespoon cashew butter
>
> 1 tablespoon curry powder
>
> 2 teaspoons sweetener of your choice
>
> 1 teaspoon onion powder
>
> ¼ teaspoon freshly ground black pepper

Pour over the prepared tofu pieces and press or squeeze it in until all the liquid is absorbed evenly (see Freezing Tofu, page 4).

Preheat the oven to 350 degrees F, and oil a 9 x 13-inch baking sheet with olive or canola oil. Arrange the tofu pieces in a single layer on the prepared baking sheet and bake for 15 minutes, or until browned on one side. Turn the pieces over and bake 10 minutes longer, or until browned on the other side.

While the tofu is baking, cook in boiling water until tender:

> ½ pound semolina or whole wheat flat noodles, linguini, or pasta of your choice

FOR THE SAUCE

Whisk together in a 2-quart saucepan:

> 3 cups water
>
> 3 tablespoons arrowroot or cornstarch
>
> 1 tablespoon vegetable broth powder

Cook over low heat, stirring or whisking constantly until thickened, being careful to avoid lumps. Stir in the baked tofu pieces and:

> ½ cup roasted cashews

Serve the hot sauce over the pasta. Sprinkle the top with:

> 2 green onions, chopped

Note: Other roasted nuts can be substituted for the cashews.

Mushroom-Almond Tofu over Pasta

Chewy frozen tofu adds texture to this flavorful dish. Use any variety of mushrooms you like.

FOR THE TOFU AND PASTA

Cut into 1½ x ½ x ½-inch pieces:

> 1 pound firm or extra-firm regular tofu, frozen, thawed, and squeezed dry

Place the tofu pieces in a 7 x 11-inch glass or stainless steel pan.

Process in a food processor or blender:

> 2 tablespoons hot water
>
> 2 tablespoons soy sauce
>
> 2 tablespoons almond butter
>
> 1 clove garlic, minced or pressed, or ½ teaspoon garlic powder
>
> ¼ teaspoon freshly ground black pepper

Pour over the prepared tofu pieces and press or squeeze it in until all the liquid is absorbed evenly (see Freezing Tofu, page 4). Preheat the oven to 350 degrees F, and oil a 9 x 13-inch baking sheet with olive or canola oil.

Arrange the tofu in a single layer on the prepared baking sheet. Bake for 15 minutes, until browned on one side. Turn the pieces over and bake 10 minutes longer, until browned on the other side.

While the tofu is baking, cook in boiling water until tender:

> 12 ounces semolina or whole wheat flat noodles or pasta of your choice

DARK MUSHROOM-ALMOND GRAVY

Heat in a large skillet or sauté pan over medium heat:

> 1 tablespoon olive oil

Cook and stir in the heated oil over medium heat until the mushrooms are soft:

> 8 ounces mushrooms, sliced
>
> ½ cup sliced almonds
>
> ¼ cup chopped fresh parsley

Whisk together:

> 3 cups water or vegetable broth
>
> 3 tablespoons arrowroot or cornstarch
>
> 1 tablespoon soy sauce

Pour into the pan with the mushrooms and almonds, and continue to cook and stir over low heat until hot and thickened, taking care to avoid lumps.

Arrange the baked tofu pieces over the cooked pasta on a platter or on plates, then pour the sauce over the top and serve.

Eggplant Lasagne

This lasagne uses breaded eggplant slices in place of pasta.

Have ready:

> 2 cups Basic Italian-Style Tomato Sauce (page 108) or other prepared tomato sauce

FOR THE EGGPLANT

Wash, peel, and slice into ¼-inch slices:

> 1 medium-size eggplant (about 1¼ pounds)

Spread the slices out on racks or paper towels. Then sprinkle with:

> 2 tablespoons freshly squeezed lemon juice
>
> 1 teaspoon salt

Let the eggplant slices stand for 5 to 10 minutes, and then wipe them dry with paper towels.

Preheat the oven to 350 degrees F, and generously oil an 11 x 17-inch baking sheet with olive oil.

While the eggplant is standing, mix together in a bowl:

> ¼ cup unbleached flour
>
> ¼ cup cornmeal
>
> ½ teaspoon ground oregano
>
> ½ teaspoon garlic powder
>
> ⅛ teaspoon freshly ground black pepper

Dredge the eggplant slices in the flour mixture and arrange them on the prepared baking sheet. Bake for 8 to 10 minutes on each side, or until golden brown.

RICOTTA-STYLE FILLING

While the eggplant slices are baking, prepare the tofu filling. Process in a food processor to a fine, grainy texture similar to ricotta cheese:

> 1½ pounds firm regular tofu
>
> ¼ cup freshly squeezed lemon juice
>
> 2 tablespoons chopped fresh basil, or 2 teaspoons dried
>
> 2 teaspoons sweetener of your choice
>
> 1 teaspoon salt
>
> 1 clove garlic, minced or pressed, or ½ teaspoon garlic powder

PUTTING IT ALL TOGETHER

Cover the bottom of an 8-inch square baking pan with 1 cup of the tomato sauce. Cover the sauce with half of the eggplant slices. Reserve ½ cup of the filling and spread the remaining filling over the eggplant. Lay the remaining eggplant slices over the filling and pour the rest of the tomato sauce over the top, spreading it evenly

Arrange the reserved tofu mixture in small dollops over the top. Bake for about 45 minutes, or until the dollops on top are lightly browned. Serve with your favorite green salad and garlic bread.

Manicotti or Herbed Stuffed Shells

Two filling choices are provided with this recipe, and either one is a winner for stuffing manicotti noodles or jumbo macaroni shells. Try making manicotti shells with homemade Spinach Noodles (page 144).

Have ready:

> 4 ounces (about 7) semolina or whole wheat manicotti noodles, 6 ounces jumbo macaroni shells, or ½ recipe Noodles or Spinach Noodles (page 144) cut to manicotti size (about seven 4 x 6-inch pieces), cooked until just tender
>
> 2 cups prepared tomato sauce or Basic Italian-Style Tomato Sauce (page 108)
>
> 1 recipe Spinach Filling or Herbed Filling (recipes follow)

SPINACH FILLING

Have ready:

> 1 pound fresh spinach, washed and chopped, or 1 package (10 ounces) frozen chopped spinach, thawed and drained

Heat in a medium-size skillet or sauté pan over low heat:

> 2 tablespoons olive oil

Cook and stir in the heated oil over low heat until translucent:

> 1 medium-size onion, chopped

Stir in the spinach, remove from the heat, and set aside.

Mix together in a bowl:

> 1 pound firm regular tofu, mashed
>
> 2 tablespoons freshly squeezed lemon juice
>
> 1 teaspoon salt
>
> ½ teaspoon garlic powder
>
> ¼ teaspoon freshly ground black pepper

Stir in the spinach mixture.

HERBED FILLING

Heat in a medium-size skillet or sauté pan over low heat:

> 1 tablespoon olive oil

Cook and stir in the heated oil over low heat until the onion is transparent:

> 1 medium-size onion, chopped
>
> ½ medium-size green bell pepper, chopped
>
> ¼ cup chopped fresh parsley

Remove from the heat and set aside.

Process in a food processor or blender until smooth and creamy:

> 1 pound firm regular tofu, mashed or crumbled
>
> 2 tablespoons freshly squeezed lemon juice
>
> 1 teaspoon salt
>
> 1 clove garlic, minced or pressed, or ½ teaspoon garlic powder
>
> 1 teaspoon minced fresh oregano, or ¼ teaspoon dried
>
> 1½ teaspoons minced fresh basil, or ½ teaspoon dried

Stir the processed tofu and cooked vegetables together.

PUTTING IT ALL TOGETHER

Preheat the oven to 350 degrees F. Pour a thin layer of the tomato sauce on the bottom of a 6 x 10-inch pan for manicotti or a 9 x 13-inch pan for shells. Fill each cooked piece of pasta equally with your choice of filling. For the homemade noodles, lay the filling across the shorter end of the noodle and roll it up. Arrange the filled pasta in the pan and cover with the rest of the tomato sauce. Cover the pan with foil to keep the noodles from drying out while baking. Bake for about 30 minutes, or until bubbling.

Lasagne

This vegan lasagne has a special creamy topping, made from soymilk and nutritional yeast, which replaces the traditional cheese. Tofu makes a creamy, cholesterol-free replacement for ricotta cheese in lasagne and similar dishes.

Have ready:

> 4 cups Basic Italian-Style Tomato Sauce (page 108) or other prepared tomato sauce
>
> 1 recipe Ricotta-Style Filling (page 105)
>
> ½ pound semolina or whole wheat lasagna noodles, cooked and drained, or oven-ready lasagna noodles

Preheat the oven to 350 degrees F. Build layers in a 9 x 13-inch lasagne pan, starting with half of the tomato sauce, then a layer of noodles, then a layer of all of the Ricotta-Style Filling, followed by a second layer of noodles, and topped with the remaining tomato sauce. Crown the lasagne with Nutritional Yeast Cheezy Sauce (recipe follows).

NUTRITIONAL YEAST CHEEZY SAUCE

Stir together with a whisk in a 2-quart saucepan:

> 2 cups unsweetened soymilk
>
> ⅓ cup nutritional yeast flakes
>
> 3 tablespoons cornstarch
>
> 1½ teaspoons Dijon mustard
>
> 1 teaspoon salt
>
> ½ teaspoon garlic powder

Bring to a boil over medium heat, whisking or stirring constantly. When the sauce starts to thicken, whisk in:

> ¼ cup olive oil

Immediately pour over the top of the lasagne. Tightly cover the pan with foil and bake for 35 to 40 minutes. Let the lasagne cool for at least 15 minutes before serving.

Greco-Italian Pasta with Tofu

This sweet-and-savory mixture of flavors along with both crunchy and soft textures makes for a unique meal.

Cook in boiling water until tender:

> 8 ounces semolina or whole wheat elbow macaroni or your favorite pasta

Have ready:

> 1 pound firm regular tofu, cut into ¼-inch cubes

Heat in a medium-size skillet or sauté pan over medium heat:

> 1 tablespoon olive oil

Brown the tofu cubes in the heated oil. Heat in a small skillet or sauté pan over low heat:

> 1 tablespoon olive oil

Simmer together in the heated oil for 1 to 2 minutes:

> ¼ cup minced fresh basil, or 1 tablespoon dried
>
> ¼ cup minced fresh parsley, or 1 tablespoon dried

> 3 tablespoons minced fresh oregano, or 1 tablespoon dried
>
> ½ teaspoon salt

Whisk together until smooth:

> 1 cup water
>
> 2 tablespoons unbleached flour, or 1 tablespoon arrowroot or cornstarch

Stir this mixture slowly into the simmering herbs and cook and stir until thickened. Remove from the heat and stir in the browned tofu along with:

> ½ cup raisins
>
> ½ cup coarsely chopped walnuts
>
> 2 cloves garlic, minced or pressed, or 1 teaspoon garlic powder

Immediately toss with the cooked pasta and serve.

Basic Italian-Style Tomato Sauce

This is a good way to sneak vegetables into children who claim they won't eat them.

Heat in a 3-quart saucepan over low heat:

> 2 tablespoons olive oil

Cook and stir in the heated oil over low heat until tender:

> 8 ounces mushrooms, sliced (optional)
>
> 1 medium-size onion, chopped
>
> 1 medium-size green bell pepper, chopped
>
> 2 carrots, diced
>
> 2 celery stalks, diced

Stir in:

> 6 cups chopped tomatoes, or 3 cans (15 ounces each) tomato sauce
>
> ½ cup chopped fresh Italian parsley
>
> 6 tablespoons minced fresh basil, or 1 tablespoon dried
>
> 2 tablespoons wine vinegar
>
> 3 cloves garlic, minced or pressed
>
> 1½ teaspoons minced fresh oregano, or ½ teaspoon dried

Simmer over low heat for 30 minutes. For a smoother texture, let the sauce cool, then process in a food processor or blender until smooth.

Portable Food

Food on the go has become the norm for our busy lifestyles. Every ethnic cuisine has some form of finger food, and tofu is an excellent choice for the protein component of the fillings in these portable foods. Many of these recipes can be made ahead and frozen for convenience. Most can also be made smaller for appetizers or for little hands.

Fajitas, page 110, with Cilantro Jalapeño Dip, page 15

Fajitas

This popular Mexican dish goes meatless with chewy frozen tofu. Fajitas are pictured on page 109.

Have ready:

> 1 pound firm or extra-firm regular tofu, frozen, thawed, and squeezed dry
>
> 4 to 6 flour tortillas (store-bought or homemade, see page 142)
>
> ½ red onion, sliced
>
> ½ red bell pepper, sliced
>
> ½ poblano or green bell pepper, sliced
>
> 2 to 3 cups chopped lettuce
>
> 1 tomato, chopped
>
> ¾ cup Cilantro-Jalapeño Dip (page 15)

Preheat the oven to 350 degrees F, and oil an 11 x 17-inch baking sheet.

FOR THE TOFU

Cut the tofu into 1 x ½ x ¼-inch pieces and place in a bowl. Mix together in another small bowl:

> ¼ cup water
>
> 2 tablespoons soy sauce
>
> 1 tablespoon natural peanut butter ·

> 1 teaspoon onion powder
>
> ½ teaspoon ground cumin
>
> ¼ teaspoon garlic powder
>
> ¼ teaspoon freshly ground black pepper

Pour over the tofu pieces and press in evenly with a spatula or your hand so the liquid is absorbed evenly (see Freezing Tofu, page 4).

Arrange the tofu in a single layer over half of the prepared baking sheet. Bake for 15 minutes, then turn the tofu over. Place the bell pepper and onion slices on the other half of the baking sheet and bake for 10 minutes longer.

PUTTING IT ALL TOGETHER

Heat each tortilla on a preheated dry griddle, just until it puffs up and is soft. Lay each hot tortilla on a plate. Divide the tofu, peppers, and onions evenly among the tortillas. Top with some of the lettuce and tomato and then a dollop (1 to 2 tablespoons) of Cilantro-Jalapeño Dip. Fold up and enjoy.

Wontons

Wontons may be deep-fried, baked, or boiled. This recipe makes enough for 85 to 90 wontons, or all the pieces in a one-pound package of commercially prepared wonton wrappers. Deep-fried or baked as a main dish, this will serve 10 to 12 people. Allow 3 or 4 wontons per serving for soups (see Watercress Soup with Wontons, page 24). Uncooked wontons may be frozen and cooked later. Cooked wontons can be frozen and reheated later.

Have ready:

> 1 package (1 pound) wonton wrappers

FOR THE FILLING

Heat in a wok, large skillet, or sauté pan over medium heat:

> 1 tablespoon canola or olive oil

Stir-fry in the heated oil for about 2 minutes, or until the vegetables are crisp-tender:

> 1 pound firm regular tofu, mashed or crumbled
>
> 1 cup shredded Chinese cabbage
>
> 1 cup fresh mung bean sprouts
>
> ¼ cup minced celery
>
> 1 tablespoon peeled and minced fresh ginger
>
> 1 tablespoon soy sauce

PUTTING IT ALL TOGETHER

There are many ways to fold a wonton—it all depends on the desired presentation. Your wonton package will show you some variations, or see the illustrations below.

One method is to place 1 teaspoon of filling in the middle of a wonton wrapper. Wet the 4 edges of the wrapper with dabs of water. Fold the wrapper in half diagonally to form a triangle,

and press the edges together. Fold it in half again, forming a long trapezoidal shape. Bring the longest ends together, then press and stick them together with a dab of water. This will form a pointed tail on the wonton.

Another method is to cut the wonton wrappers into circles. You can cut several at a time with scissors or a sharp knife. Place 1 teaspoon of filling in the lower half of the circle. Fold the top half over and seal it with a dab of water. Take the two corners of the resulting half circle and bring them around to meet each other, pressing them together with a dab of water to make them stick.

To deep-fry: Heat canola or peanut oil to 365 to 368 degrees F and deep-fry the wontons a few at a time, maintaining the heat, until golden brown. Drain on absorbent paper and serve.

To oven-fry: Preheat the oven to 350 degrees F, and oil several 11 x 17-inch baking sheets. Place the wontons on the prepared baking sheets, and spray the tops with a little more canola oil. Bake for about 5 minutes, or until browned.

To boil: Drop the wontons in boiling water or soup during the last 5 minutes of cooking.

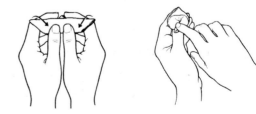

Spring Rolls

Choose from the two filling options provided or make up your own with what you have on hand. Spring rolls can be oven-fried or deep-fried. Serve them as a main dish or make them smaller for appetizers. Be sure to have all the ingredients ready before you begin to cook.

Have ready:

> 12 to 15 spring roll wrappers
>
> 1 recipe Spring Roll Filling 1 or 2 (recipes follow)

SPRING ROLL FILLING 1

Place in a glass or stainless steel pan or bowl:

> 1 pound firm or extra-firm regular tofu, cut into small strips or cubes

To make the marinade, chop together in a food processor:

> 1 piece (1-inch cube) peeled fresh ginger
>
> 2 cloves garlic

Add and process with the chopped garlic and ginger:

> 2 tablespoons soy sauce
>
> 2 tablespoons mirin

Pour over the tofu, cover, and marinate in the refrigerator while you prepare the vegetables.

Place in separate bowls:

> 1 cup sliced mushrooms
>
> 1 small bell pepper (any color), thinly sliced
>
> 1 stalk celery, thinly sliced on the diagonal
>
> 2 green onions, chopped
>
> 3 cups shredded cabbage
>
> 1½ cups chopped bok choy

Heat a wok, large skillet, or sauté pan over medium heat and add:

> 1 tablespoon canola or peanut oil

Immediately add the mushrooms, bell pepper, celery, and green onions to the hot wok and cook and stir for 2 minutes.

Add the cabbage, bok choy, and tofu, cover, and steam for 4 minutes. Stir, then cover and steam for 4 minutes longer. Stir again and remove from the heat.

SPRING ROLL FILLING 2

Have ready:

> 1 pound firm or extra-firm tofu, frozen, thawed, squeezed dry, and cut into small strips or cubes

Chop together in a food processor or by hand:

> 1 piece (1-inch cube) peeled fresh ginger
>
> 1 clove garlic

Add and stir or process:

> 2 tablespoons soy sauce
>
> 1 tablespoon rice vinegar

Pour over the tofu pieces in a bowl and gently squeeze it in, pressing evenly with a spatula or your hand (see Freezing Tofu, page 4).

Place in separate bowls:

> 1 cup snow peas, cut into 1-inch pieces (about ¼ pound)
>
> 6 ounces mushrooms, sliced
>
> ½ cup chopped green onions
>
> 3 cups mung bean sprouts
>
> 1 cup chopped bok choy leaves
>
> ½ cup minced water chestnuts

Heat a wok over medium heat and add:

1 tablespoon canola or peanut oil

Immediately add the snow peas, mushrooms, and green onions and cook and stir for 2 minutes.

Add and stir in the tofu, bean sprouts, bok choy, and water chestnuts. Cover and steam for 4 minutes longer. Stir well and remove from the heat.

PUTTING IT ALL TOGETHER

To prepare each spring roll, place ⅓ to ½ cup of filling in the center of each wrapper. Bring 1 corner over and tuck it around the filling, then fold the 2 side corners over on top. Roll it over and secure the top flap with a dab of water.

To oven-fry: Preheat the oven to 400 degrees F. Spray a nonstick 11 x 17-inch baking sheet with canola oil, and arrange the spring rolls an equal distance apart. Spray the top of the rolls with canola oil and bake for 5 to 7 minutes, or until golden brown on the bottom. Turn them over and bake for 5 to 7 minutes longer to brown the other side.

To deep-fry: Carefully place two rolls at a time in peanut or canola oil preheated to 365 to 368 degrees F, and fry until golden brown on one side. Carefully roll the spring rolls over to brown on the other side. If the oil temperature is maintained, the rolls will brown without absorbing much oil. Do not let the oil smoke. Drain on absorbent paper.

Serve the hot spring rolls with Sweet-and-Sour Sauce (page 92), Chinese hot mustard, or soy sauce.

Mediterranean Spring Rolls

These rolls are an adaptation of the Greek dish spanakopita, in individual servings. Serve them as a main dish or make the rolls smaller for appetizers. Be sure to follow the package directions for thawing and using the phyllo dough.

Have ready:

> 1 package phyllo dough, thawed
>
> 2 tablespoons olive oil

FOR THE FILLING

Mix together in a large bowl:

> 1 pound firm regular tofu, mashed or crumbled
>
> 1 bunch fresh spinach, washed, stemmed, and chopped (about 4 cups)
>
> ½ cup minced green onions
>
> ¼ cup freshly squeezed lemon juice
>
> 2 tablespoons minced fresh mint, or 2 teaspoons dried
>
> 1 tablespoon minced fresh basil, or 1 teaspoon dried
>
> 1 clove garlic, minced or pressed, or ½ teaspoon garlic powder
>
> 1 teaspoon salt
>
> ½ teaspoon freshly ground black pepper

Preheat the oven to 350 degrees F, and lightly oil an 11 x 17-inch baking sheet.

PUTTING IT ALL TOGETHER

To make each roll, fold 1 sheet of phyllo dough in half and brush it lightly with some of the olive oil. Fold it in half again to form about a 4-inch square and place ⅓ to ½ cup of filling in the middle. Fold the four corners together like an envelope. Place the folded side down on the prepared baking sheet and brush the top lightly with some of the olive oil. Repeat the process with the remaining phyllo dough and filling to make 12 to 15 rolls. Bake the rolls for about 20 minutes, or until lightly browned.

Taquitos

Taquitos are classic Mexican fare, usually filled with flavored meat and deep-fried. The chewy texture of flavored frozen tofu works perfectly here in concert with avocado sauce and chiles. For appetizers, make taquitos with smaller (three-inch) corn tortillas.

Have ready:

> 24 corn tortillas
>
> 1½ pounds firm to extra-firm regular tofu, frozen, thawed, squeezed dry, and torn into bite-size pieces

FOR THE AVOCADO SAUCE

Peel and mash:

> 2 ripe Hass avocados

Stir in:

> 1 cup green taco sauce, or 1 to 2 minced chipotles en adobo or jalapeño chiles
>
> 2 tablespoons freshly squeezed lime juice
>
> 2 cloves garlic, minced or pressed, or 1 teaspoon garlic powder

Chill for 1 hour before serving.

FOR THE FILLING

Mix together:

> 3 tablespoons soy sauce
>
> 2 tablespoons natural peanut butter
>
> 6 cloves garlic, pressed

Pour over the tofu pieces in a bowl and press with a spatula or your hand so the mixture is evenly absorbed (see Freezing Tofu, page 4).

Stir in:

> 1 cup diced onion

Heat in large skillet or sauté pan over low heat:

> 2 tablespoons canola or light olive oil

Brown the tofu mixture in the heated oil over medium heat, then set aside.

The tortillas need to be soft and flexible to roll easily. If you don't have access to freshly made tortillas, soften them on a hot griddle or *comal* for a few seconds, or place them in a single layer in the microwave for 5 to 10 seconds.

Spoon 2 to 2½ tablespoons of filling across each softened tortilla, then roll the tortilla snugly around the filling. If necessary, weave a wooden toothpick from end to end through each taquito to keep it closed.

To pan-fry: Pour about ¾ inch of canola oil into a heavy skillet and preheat it to 365 to 368 degrees F. Carefully add and fry 3 taquitos at a time. When they are golden brown on one side, turn them over and fry until golden brown on the other side. Drain on absorbent paper.

To oven-fry: Preheat the oven to 350 degrees F, and oil an 11 x 17-inch baking sheet. Arrange the taquitos on the prepared baking sheet and spray the tops lightly with canola oil. Bake for 8 to 10 minutes on each side, or until crisp.

Remove the toothpicks and serve with the avocado sauce and chopped fresh cilantro. Taquitos can also be served with refried pinto or black beans, Spanish or Mexican rice, and your favorite tossed green salad.

VARIATIONS

Taquitos with Potatoes: Add 1 cup of diced potatoes and brown them with the onions for the filling.

Taquitos with Poblanos: Stir into the browned filling 1 to 2 roasted poblano chiles that have been peeled, seeded, and cut into thin strips.

Tofu Turnovers

Turnovers are great finger food, hot or cold, for lunch boxes or picnics. They can also be frozen and reheated later. Make them mini size for appetizers. Vary the filling to suit your taste.

FOR THE DOUGH

Stir together in a large bowl:

> 1½ cups warm potato cooking water (110 to 115 degrees F)
>
> ½ cup mashed potatoes
>
> 2 tablespoons olive or canola oil
>
> 1 tablespoon active dry yeast
>
> 1 tablespoon sweetener of your choice

Let rise for 10 minutes, and then mix in gradually:

> 3½ to 4 cups whole wheat flour
>
> 3½ to 4 cups unbleached flour
>
> 1 teaspoon salt

Knead the dough until smooth and not sticky. Cover the bowl and let the dough rise in a warm place while you prepare the filling.

FOR THE FILLING

Heat in a large skillet or sauté pan over low heat:

> 1 tablespoon olive oil

Cook and stir in the heated oil over medium heat until the vegetables are crisp-tender:

> 3 medium-size carrots, thinly sliced
>
> 3 stalks celery, thinly sliced
>
> 1 medium-size onion, chopped
>
> 1 small green bell pepper, chopped
>
> 3 cloves garlic, minced

Stir in during the last minute of cooking:

> ¾ cup chopped snow peas or fresh or frozen green peas
>
> 1 teaspoon salt

When the vegetables are crisp-tender, remove from the heat and stir in:

> 1½ pounds firm regular tofu, mashed or chopped

PUTTING IT ALL TOGETHER

Preheat the oven to 425 degrees F, and oil one or two 11 x 17-inch baking sheets.

Divide the dough into 18 balls, about 2 inches in diameter, then roll out each ball into a 6-inch circle on a floured board. Alternatively, roll the dough out to ⅛ inch thick and cut it into 18 (6-inch) squares. Put 2 to 3 tablespoons of the turnover filling in the center of each circle or square (see illustrations below). Moisten the edges with water, fold over, and seal by pressing the edges together with a fork.

Place the turnovers on the prepared baking sheets and bake for about 15 minutes, or until lightly browned. Be careful—they burn easily. Serve the turnovers in a cloth-lined basket to keep them warm.

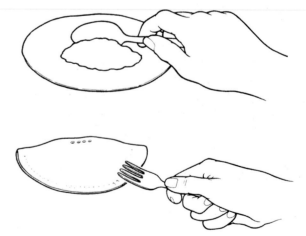

Tofu Knishes

Knishes make great portable food and can be made smaller to be served as an appetizer. Have the horseradish and mustard ready!

FOR THE DOUGH

Beat together in a large bowl:

- 1 cup mashed potatoes
- 1 tablespoon olive oil
- 1 teaspoon salt

Mix together in a separate large bowl:

- 3 cups unbleached flour, or 1½ cups whole wheat and 1½ cups unbleached flour
- 1 teaspoon baking powder

Stir in the potato mixture until it starts to form a ball. Stir in and knead into a smooth dough:

- ½ cup cold water

Let the dough rest on a board, covered with a cloth, for 30 minutes.

FOR THE FILLING

Heat in a medium-size skillet or sauté pan over low heat:

- 2 tablespoons olive oil

Cook and stir in the heated oil over low heat until caramelized:

- 1 cup chopped onion

Put the caramelized onion in a large bowl and stir together with:

- 1½ cups mashed potatoes
- ¾ pound firm regular tofu, mashed
- ¼ cup chopped fresh parsley
- 1 teaspoon salt
- 2 cloves garlic, minced or pressed, or 1 teaspoon garlic powder
- ¼ teaspoon freshly ground black pepper

PUTTING IT ALL TOGETHER

Preheat the oven to 350 degrees F, and oil an 11 x 17-inch baking sheet.

Cut the dough into 4 equal sections. Roll each section as thinly as possible on a floured surface to about 1/16 inch thick. Cut the rolled dough into 5 x 6-inch rectangles and place 2 to 3 tablespoons of the filling in the middle of each one. Fold the sides in first, then the ends (as illustrated below). This will make 12 (3 x 4-inch) knishes. Place the folded side down on the prepared baking sheet. Bake the knishes for 25 minutes, or until golden. Serve with horseradish or mustard.

Counterclockwise from top: Summer Vegetable Medley, Penne Rigate with Red Pepper Sauce, and Risotto Verde

side d

Side Dishes

Side dishes are meant to complement, complete, and bolster the main dish of a meal. "Do you want fries with that?" does not apply here. Whether based on vegetables or grains, these side dishes are fortified with protein and other healthful nutrients from tofu. Diversity reigns in these recipes, with flavors derived from different cultural cuisines.

Summer Vegetable Medley

Summer harvest time brings a bounty of fresh vegetables and herbs for the table, which was the inspiration for this colorful dish. This recipe is pictured on page 118.

Have ready:

> 1 pound firm regular tofu, frozen, thawed, squeezed dry, and cubed

Heat in a wok, large skillet, or sauté pan over low heat:

> 1 tablespoon olive oil

Cook and stir in the heated oil over medium heat until the onion and pepper start to soften:

> 1 red onion, chopped
> 1 red bell pepper, chopped
> 1 large clove garlic, minced

Add the tofu and cook and stir until lightly browned. Then add and continue to cook and stir until well combined:

> 1 pound plum tomatoes, peeled and chopped
> 1 small zucchini, sliced
> 1 small yellow squash, sliced
> 1 cup cut green beans
> 1 cup fresh corn kernels
> ¼ cup chopped fresh basil leaves, packed
> 3 tablespoons minced fresh parsley
> 1 teaspoon salt
> ½ teaspoon freshly ground black pepper

Cover and steam over low heat until the vegetables are crisp-tender.

Cumin Potatoes with Tofu

This makes a great side dish for Indian entrées like curried dal (peas, beans, or lentils) and brown rice.

Have ready:

> 2 pounds waxy potatoes, steamed until tender, cooled, peeled, and cubed
> ½ pound carrots, cubed and steamed until tender
> ½ pound fresh or thawed frozen green peas

Heat in a large skillet or sauté pan over low heat:

> ¼ cup canola or coconut oil

Stir in and let sizzle in the hot oil for 3 to 4 seconds, or until the mustard seeds starts to pop:

> 1 tablespoon cumin seeds
> 1 tablespoon brown mustard seeds
> ½ to 1 teaspoon crushed red pepper flakes

Add to the seed mixture and cook and stir until translucent:

> 1 onion, chopped

Add:

> ½ pound firm regular tofu, cubed

Cook and stir until the tofu starts to brown. Then stir in the potatoes, onions, peas, and:

> 1 teaspoon salt

Continue to cook and stir until everything is heated through, taking care it does not stick to the bottom of the pan.

Thai Tofu Peanut Sauce with Veggies

MAKES 4 TO 6 SERVINGS

Here are Thai-inspired vegetables in a spicy, creamy tofu sauce.

TOFU PEANUT SAUCE

Makes 1½ cups

Chop in a food processor:

> ½ cup dry-roasted peanuts
> ¼ cup soy sauce
> ¼ cup freshly squeezed lime juice or rice vinegar
> 2 tablespoons sweetener of your choice
> 1 small jalapeño chile
> 1½ tablespoons chopped fresh basil
> 1 piece (1-inch cube) fresh ginger
> 2 cloves garlic

Add and process until smooth and creamy:

> ½ pound firm regular tofu, mashed or crumbled

The sauce can be heated gently (do not boil) or served at room temperature.

FOR THE VEGETABLES

Cook and stir in a small amount of heated oil or steam until crisp-tender:

> 2 to 3 pounds fresh or frozen mixed vegetables (if fresh, cut into equal bite-size chunks)

Pour the sauce over the hot vegetables and top with chopped fresh cilantro.

VARIATION

Serve the vegetables and sauce over mung bean threads, rice sticks, or hot rice.

Penne Rigate WITH SWEET RED PEPPER SAUCE

MAKES 6 TO 8 SERVINGS

"Penne rigate" refers to tube pasta with ridges. This dish, with its creamy red sauce and pasta, is striking. It is pictured on page 118.

Cook in boiling water until tender:

> 1 pound whole wheat or semolina penne rigate or pasta of your choice

Drain in a colander and set aside but keep warm. Heat in a large skillet or sauté pan over low heat:

> 1 tablespoon olive oil

Cook and stir in the heated oil over medium heat until soft:

> 2 medium-size carrots, thinly sliced
> 1 large onion, chopped
> 1 large red bell pepper, chopped
> 3 tablespoons minced fresh basil, or
> 1 tablespoon dried

> 1 large clove garlic, minced

Transfer the cooked vegetables to a food processor and add:

> 1 package (12.3 ounces) silken tofu, mashed or crumbled

Process until smooth and creamy. Pour into a saucepan and stir in:

> 1 teaspoon salt
> ¼ teaspoon freshly ground black pepper

Warm gently over medium heat. Serve the heated sauce over the warm pasta.

SIDE DISHES   121

Scalloped Cabbage

Creamy blended tofu is combined with crisp-tender cabbage and savory onions for this classic side dish.

Parboil in 1 cup boiling water for 5 minutes:

> **4 cups coarsely chopped cabbage**

Heat in a large skillet or sauté pan over low heat:

> **2 tablespoons olive oil**

Cook and stir in the heated oil over low heat until soft:

> **1 large onion, chopped**

Sprinkle over the onion:

> **2 tablespoons unbleached flour**
>
> **½ teaspoon salt**

Drain the cabbage cooking water into the onion mixture. Cook and stir over low heat until thick.

Preheat the oven to 350 degrees F. Process in a blender or food processor until smooth and creamy:

> **½ pound soft regular tofu, mashed or crumbled**
>
> **2 tablespoons apple cider vinegar**
>
> **1 teaspoon salt**
>
> **⅛ teaspoon freshly ground black pepper**

Stir into the cabbage along with the onion mixture. Pour into 1½-quart baking dish, top with dried bread crumbs, and sprinkle with paprika. Bake for 30 minutes, or until browned on top.

Chilaquiles

This is a version of a classic Mexican dish that makes use of day-old corn tortillas.

Cut or tear into bite-size pieces:

> **24 corn tortillas**

Mix in a medium-size bowl and set aside:

> **½ pound medium-firm tofu, crumbled**
>
> **1 jar (8 ounces) mild to hot tomato salsa**
>
> **3 small cloves garlic, pressed**

Heat in a large skillet or wok over medium heat:

> **2 tablespoons canola or light olive oil**

Add the tortilla pieces to the heated oil and cook and stir over medium heat until they are evenly coated with the oil. Add to the skillet and continue to cook and stir until the tortillas and onion are browned:

> **1 medium-size onion, chopped**

Sprinkle with:

> **1 teaspoon salt**

Stir the tofu mixture into the skillet. Cover and steam for 2 to 3 minutes, or until hot.

Stuffed Baked Tomatoes

Stuffed Baked Tomatoes are pictured below.

Cut or scoop out a hollow on the stem end of:

> 8 large or 12 small ripe tomatoes

Remove the seeds, leaving about two-thirds of the tomato a hollow receptacle.

Heat in a medium-size skillet or sauté pan over low heat:

> 2 tablespoons olive oil

Cook and stir in the heated oil over medium heat until soft:

> 1 cup diced onion
> ½ cup diced green bell pepper

Remove from the heat and set aside. Preheat the oven to 400 degrees F, and oil a 9-inch square baking pan.

Mix together in a medium-size bowl:

> 1 pound firm regular tofu, mashed
> ¼ cup minced fresh parley
> 1 tablespoon soy sauce
> 1 clove garlic, minced or pressed, or ½ teaspoon garlic powder

Stir the onion and bell pepper into the tofu mixture, and then spoon it into the hollow of the prepared tomatoes. Place the stuffed tomatoes in the prepared baking pan. Top each one with a sprinkle of dried bread crumbs or cracker crumbs. Bake for 20 minutes, or until browned on top. Serve hot or chilled.

Stuffed Baked Tomatoes

Walnut-Stuffed Zucchini

These stuffed zucchini can be enjoyed at harvest time or any time of year.

Preheat the oven to 375 degrees F, and oil a 9 x 13-inch baking pan. Wash and trim the ends off:

4 small zucchini (about 1½ pounds)

Cut the zucchini in half lengthwise and scoop out the seed pulp. Chop and set aside the seed pulp to add to the stuffing. Parboil the zucchini shells for 1 minute and drain. Alternatively, place them on an oiled baking sheet and roast them in the preheated oven for 15 minutes, or until crisp-tender.

Heat in a large skillet or sauté pan over low heat:

1 tablespoon olive oil

Cook and stir together over low heat until transparent:

⅓ cup chopped onion

1 clove garlic, minced

Mash in a large bowl:

½ pound firm regular tofu

Stir in the chopped zucchini pulp, the cooked onion, and:

⅓ cup chopped walnuts

¼ cup chopped fresh basil

2 tablespoons red wine vinegar or apple cider vinegar

1½ tablespoons sweet white miso, or 1 teaspoon salt

1 tablespoon ground flaxseeds

⅛ teaspoon freshly ground black pepper

Heap the filling into the zucchini shells, sprinkle with paprika, and arrange in the prepared baking pan. Bake for 15 to 20 minutes, or until browned on top.

Note: If you have leftover filling, try stuffing pre-roasted multicolored bell pepper halves. Roast the pepper halves at 375 degrees F for about 15 minutes, stuff with the filling, and return to the oven for about 15 minutes longer.

This savory fried rice makes a great side dish for almost any entrée.

Have ready:

> 4 cups cooked brown or white rice, at room temperature

Heat in a heavy skillet or wok over low heat:

> 1 tablespoon olive or canola oil

Cook and stir in the heated oil over low heat:

> 2 cloves garlic, crushed with the side of a knife or cleaver

Cook until the garlic is light brown, then remove and discard it.

Cook and stir in the hot oil for 1 minute over medium heat:

> ¾ pound firm regular tofu, diced

While the tofu is cooking, sprinkle it with:

> 1 tablespoon soy sauce

Remove the tofu from skillet and set it aside.

Add to the hot skillet:

> 1 tablespoon olive or canola oil
>
> 2 cloves garlic, minced

Cook and stir for 1 minute over medium heat, then add:

> 1½ cups diced onion
>
> 1 cup diced celery

Cook and stir for 2 to 3 minutes. Add the cooked rice and cook and stir until everything is evenly mixed. Gently stir in the prepared tofu and:

> 1½ cups fresh mung bean sprouts

Gently cook and stir for 2 minutes longer, sprinkling with:

> 1 tablespoon soy sauce

Gently stir again. Serve hot, topped with chopped green onions.

Tofu Fried Rice

125

Java Tofu Pilaf

Inspired by spicy-sweet Javanese cuisine, this pilaf makes a unique rice side dish.

Have ready:

> ¾ pound firm to extra-firm regular tofu, cut into ½-inch cubes

Mix together until smooth:

> 2 tablespoons soy sauce
>
> 1 tablespoon natural peanut butter

Pour over the tofu cubes and mix well. Heat in a large skillet or sauté pan over medium heat:

> 1 tablespoon olive or canola oil

Brown the tofu cubes in the heated oil. Heat in a medium-size skillet over low heat:

> 1 tablespoon olive or canola oil

Cook and stir in the heated oil over low heat:

> 1 medium-size onion, chopped

When the onion becomes limp, add:

> ½ cup brown or white rice
>
> ¼ cup raisins
>
> 1 tablespoon curry powder
>
> 1 teaspoon salt
>
> ¼ teaspoon ground coriander
>
> ¼ teaspoon ground cumin

Stir and toast the rice mixture over medium heat for 5 minutes. Then pour in:

> 1¾ cups boiling water or vegetable broth

Stir in the browned tofu, bring to a boil, stir, cover, and simmer over low heat for 45 minutes for brown rice or 20 minutes for white rice.

Tofu Kartoffelkuchen

These savory, German-inspired potato cakes make a hearty breakfast, appetizer, brunch, or side dish. Be sure to use a starchy potato like russets. Tofu Kartoffelkuchen is pictured on the opposite page.

Stir together in a large bowl:

> 8 medium-size potatoes, grated
>
> ½ pound soft regular tofu, processed in a blender until smooth
>
> 1 large onion, grated
>
> ¼ cup minced fresh parsley
>
> 3 tablespoons unbleached flour
>
> 1 teaspoon salt
>
> 2 cloves garlic, minced or pressed, or 1 teaspoon garlic powder
>
> ¼ teaspoon freshly ground black pepper

Heat a 6-inch skillet over medium heat and brush with light olive or canola oil. Spoon about ¾ cup of the potato mixture into the pan and flatten it to about ½ inch thick. Fry over medium heat for 5 to 7 minutes on each side, or until golden brown. Brush more oil on the pan for the second side, if needed. Repeat this process for the remaining potato mixture; it should make 8 (6-inch) cakes. Serve hot with applesauce on the side, or top with Tofu Sour Creamy Dressing (page 50).

Risotto Verde

MAKES 6 TO 8 SERVINGS

For more variety, try this tasty dish with millet or quinoa in place of rice. See a photo of this recipe using rice on page 118.

Have ready:

> 2 cups cooked brown or white rice or other cooked grain of your choice

Preheat the oven to 325 degrees F, and oil a 1½-quart glass baking dish.

Prepare and set aside:

> 2 cups chopped dark leafy greens (such as spinach, kale, or other favorites), uncooked, or
> 1 package (10 ounces) frozen chopped spinach, thawed and drained (reserve the liquid)

Process in a blender or food processor until smooth and creamy:

> ½ pound firm regular tofu, mashed or crumbled
> 4 to 6 tablespoons water or liquid from the thawed spinach, as needed to facilitate blending

> 1½ teaspoons salt

Heat in a large skillet or sauté pan over low heat:

> 1 tablespoon olive oil

Cook and stir in the heated oil over low heat until caramelized:

> 1 medium-size onion, finely chopped
> 2 cloves garlic, minced

Remove from the heat and fold in the cooked rice, chopped greens, blended tofu mixture, and:

> ¼ teaspoon freshly ground black pepper
> ⅛ teaspoon freshly grated nutmeg

Spoon the mixture into the prepared baking dish and spread it out evenly. Bake for about 30 minutes.

Tofu Kartoffelkuchen

This rice ring is especially attractive when filled with steamed or stir-fried vegetables.

Have ready:

> 4 cups cooked brown or white rice

Place in a bowl:

> 1 pound firm regular tofu, cut into ½-inch cubes

Whisk together in a small bowl or process in a blender:

> ¼ cup soy sauce
>
> 2 tablespoons natural peanut butter
>
> 1 teaspoon onion powder
>
> ¼ teaspoon garlic powder

Pour over the tofu cubes and gently stir until all the cubes are evenly coated. Heat in a large skillet or sauté pan over low heat:

> 1 tablespoon olive oil

Brown the coated tofu cubes in the heated oil over medium heat, then set aside. Heat in a medium-size skillet or sauté pan over low heat:

> 1 tablespoon olive oil

Cook and stir in the heated oil until crisp-tender, then set aside:

> 1 large stalk celery, diced
>
> 4 green onions, cut into ½-inch pieces

Preheat the oven to 400 degrees F, and generously oil a 5- to 6-cup ring mold.

Process in a blender or food processor until smooth and creamy:

> ¼ pound soft regular tofu, mashed or crumbled (½ cup)
>
> ⅛ teaspoon freshly ground black pepper

In a large bowl, gently fold together the cooked vegetables, browned tofu, cooked rice, and blended tofu with:

> ½ cup sliced kalamata or black olives
>
> ¼ cup chopped pimientos or roasted red bell peppers

Press the mixture firmly into the prepared ring mold. Fit the ring mold inside another baking pan that has 1 inch of boiling water in the bottom, and bake for 20 to 25 minutes, or until lightly browned on top.

Remove the ring mold from the oven and let cool for 5 minutes. Loosen the edges with the flat side of a table knife and turn out onto a platter. Fill the center of the ring with steamed or stir-fried vegetables.

Corn Pie

This is a Southwestern-inspired side-dish casserole using both whole corn kernels and cornmeal.

Preheat the oven to 350 degrees F, and oil a 6½ x 10-inch (2 quart) pan or casserole dish.

FOR THE FILLING

Heat in a wok, large skillet, or sauté pan over low heat:

> 1 tablespoon olive or canola oil

Cook and stir in the heated oil over medium heat until transparent:

> 1 medium-size onion, chopped

Add and cook and stir for 5 minutes:

> ¾ pound firm regular tofu, crumbled
>
> 1 to 2 teaspoons chili powder
>
> ¼ teaspoon freshly ground black pepper
>
> Dash of cayenne

Then add:

> 1 can (17 ounces) corn kernels, drained, or 2 cups frozen corn kernels, thawed
>
> 18 pitted black olives, cut in half
>
> ½ cup water

Cook and stir until everything is heated through. Pour into the prepared pan and set aside.

FOR THE TOPPING

Mix together in a medium-size bowl:

> ¾ cup cornmeal
>
> ¼ cup unbleached or whole wheat pastry flour
>
> 1 tablespoon sweetener of your choice (if using a liquid sweetener, add it to the soymilk)
>
> 1 teaspoon baking powder
>
> ½ teaspoon salt
>
> ¼ teaspoon baking soda

Mix together in a measuring cup or small bowl:

> ¾ cup unsweetened soymilk
>
> 2 tablespoons canola or olive oil

Pour into the flour mixture and stir until everything is just moistened. Pour over the top of the tofu mixture in the pan and spread it out evenly. Bake for about 25 minutes, or until the topping is golden.

Try stuffing red, yellow, orange, green, and purple bell peppers for a colorful presentation.

Place in a glass or stainless steel bowl:

> 1 pound firm regular tofu, cut into 1 x ½ x ¼-inch pieces

Whisk together in a small bowl:

> 3 tablespoons soy sauce
>
> 3 tablespoons natural peanut butter
>
> 2 teaspoons onion powder
>
> ½ teaspoon garlic powder

Pour over the tofu pieces and gently stir until evenly coated. Cover and marinate in the refrigerator for 30 minutes.

Heat in a medium-size skillet or sauté pan over low heat:

> 2 tablespoons olive oil

Brown the marinated tofu pieces in the heated oil over medium heat, then set aside.

Wash and cut off the tops of:

> 6 large bell peppers (any color)

Remove the stems, membranes, and seeds, and set aside the tops to chop for the filling. Parboil the peppers in 1 inch of boiling water for 5 minutes. Alternatively, preheat the oven to 375 degrees F, place the peppers on a baking sheet, and roast them for 15 minutes.

Preheat the oven to 400 degrees F, and oil a 7 x 11-inch baking dish. Arrange the peppers in the prepared dish.

For the filling, heat in a large skillet or sauté pan over low heat:

> 2 tablespoons olive oil

Cook and stir in the heated oil over medium heat until soft:

> 1 large onion, chopped
>
> 6 bell pepper tops, chopped
>
> 2 stalks celery, chopped
>
> 2 cloves garlic, minced

Stir in:

> 1 tablespoon chili powder
>
> 1 tablespoon minced fresh oregano, or ½ teaspoon dried
>
> 1 teaspoon ground cumin

Cook for 1 minute over medium heat. Then stir in the browned tofu and:

> 1½ cups corn kernels
>
> 1 cup tomato sauce

Cook until heated through. Stuff the peppers with the filling, then pour over them:

> 1 cup tomato sauce

Bake for about 25 minutes.

Note: If you prefer, the peppers can be cut in half lengthwise before parboiling or roasting and stuffing. Arrange them in an oiled 9 x 13-inch pan and bake as directed.

Spinach Soufflé or Timbale

Tofu replaces eggs in this savory baked dish with a custardlike texture. For a festive presentation, try making this in a timbale ring mold if you have one.

Have ready:

> 1 package (10 ounces) frozen chopped spinach, thawed and drained (reserve the liquid), or 2 cups chopped fresh spinach, packed

Preheat the oven to 350 degrees F, and oil an 8-inch round or square baking pan or timbale ring mold.

To make the base sauce, heat in a large skillet over low heat:

> 2 tablespoons olive oil

Cook and stir in the heated oil over low heat until limp:

> ½ cup chopped onion

Stir in:

> 3 tablespoons unbleached flour
>
> 1 cup liquid (use the thawed spinach liquid and water or unsweetened soymilk)

> ½ teaspoon salt
>
> Dash of freshly ground black pepper
>
> Dash of freshly grated nutmeg

Fold the prepared spinach into the sauce.

Process in a food processor or blender until smooth and creamy:

> ½ pound soft regular tofu, mashed or crumbled
>
> 2 tablespoons freshly squeezed lemon juice or apple cider vinegar
>
> ½ teaspoon salt
>
> Dash of freshly ground black pepper

Fold the blended mixture into the base sauce. Pour into the prepared baking pan and bake for 30 minutes, or until set and small cracks start to form on the edges.

Potato Bread and Rolls, Cinnamon Rolls, Flour Tortillas, Sesame Tofu Crackers, and Hush Puppies

brea

Breads

Homemade breads have some of the most alluring aromas in the kitchen. Tofu can be added to bread dough or batter or used as the base for a creamy filling. It increases the protein and makes a moister crumb. Using whole grain flours will further boost the nutritional value of breads. Due to its amazing adaptability, tofu can even replace eggs in many conventional bread recipes. In this section you'll find recipes for yeast breads, quick breads, tortillas, and noodles. Whether you use an electric mixer or stir and knead by hand, these recipes are well worth the effort. If you have a bread machine, be sure to follow the directions in the instruction manual that came with it in order to adapt these recipes.

Focaccia with Tofu

Focaccia is best baked on a baking stone, but if necessary you can use a baking sheet. It can be made thick or thin, soft or crisp, according to your preference. Focaccia with Tofu is pictured on the opposite page.

Combine in a food processor with a dough blade or in a mixer with dough hook:

⅔ cup warm water (105 to 115 degrees F)

1 tablespoon sweetener of your choice

1 teaspoon active dry yeast

Let stand until the mixture starts to foam. Then beat in:

½ pound soft regular tofu (at room temperature), mashed or blended

Add and beat in until the mixture forms a smooth ball and cleans the sides of the bowl:

2½ to 3 cups bread flour or whole wheat flour

2 tablespoons olive oil

1 teaspoon salt

Add more flour as needed to clean the sides of the bowl. Transfer the dough to a lightly floured surface. Knead until smooth and elastic. Place in a large, warm oiled bowl and turn the dough once so it is coated all over with oil. Cover the bowl with a clean dry cloth or plastic wrap and let rest about 15 minutes.

Divide the dough in half or thirds. Sprinkle 1 to 3 baking sheets with cornmeal (depending on the size of the sheets). Roll or press out by hand each piece of dough on a prepared baking sheet to form an 8-inch round. Cover loosely with a clean dry cloth or plastic wrap and let rise until slightly puffed. Brush the tops with:

1 to 2 tablespoons olive oil

Arrange your choice of toppings on the puffed dough:

Chopped fresh basil

Roma tomatoes, sliced

Tofu, crumbled and mixed with soy Parmesan

10 to 15 pitted kalamata olives, sliced in half lengthwise

3 tablespoons finely chopped fresh sage, or 1 tablespoon dried

1 tablespoon chopped fresh rosemary, or 1½ teaspoons dried

Preheat the oven to 475 degrees F. Transfer the focaccias to a preheated baking stone or bake them directly on the baking sheets. Bake for 10 to 15 minutes, or until golden brown. Transfer to racks to cool slightly. Serve warm.

This makes light, soft bread or rolls. Potato Bread and Rolls and Cinnamon Rolls are pictured on page 132.

Boil in 1 inch of water until soft:

> 3 medium-size potatoes

Remove the potatoes and set aside the cooking water. Mash the potatoes and measure out 1½ cups. Store any extra mashed potatoes in the refrigerator to use in another recipe. Dissolve together in a large bowl:

> 1 cup warm potato water (105 to 115 degrees F)
>
> 2 tablespoons active dry yeast
>
> 1 tablespoon sweetener of your choice

Let stand for 10 minutes, or until foamy. Process in a blender or food processor until smooth and creamy:

> 1½ cups mashed potatoes, cooled
>
> ½ pound soft regular tofu, mashed or crumbled
>
> 1 cup warm water

Stir the tofu mixture into the foamy yeast mixture. Then stir in:

> 4 cups unbleached flour
>
> ½ cup canola or coconut oil
>
> 1 tablespoon salt

Beat well; the dough will be soft. Cover and let rise in a warm place for 20 minutes.

Stir the dough down. Add and stir in until the dough starts to form a ball:

> 3 to 4 cups unbleached flour

Preheat the oven to 375 degrees F, and oil 2 bread pans or baking sheets. Knead the dough into a smooth, soft ball. Form into 2 loaves or about 36 rolls. Place in the prepared bread pans (for bread) or on the prepared baking sheets (for rolls). Cover with a towel and let rise in a warm place for about 20 minutes, or until almost double in bulk.

Bake the loaves for 40 minutes, or bake the rolls for 20 minutes, until golden brown.

VARIATION

Cinnamon Rolls (makes about 36 rolls): Preheat the oven to 375 degrees F, and oil 2 baking sheets. After kneading the dough into a smooth, soft ball, divide it in half and roll out each half on a well-floured board into a large rectangle about ¼ inch thick. Prepare the Cinnamon Roll Filling (recipe follows), then sprinkle and spread half the filling over all of the rolled-out dough. Roll up each rectangle of dough jelly-roll style. Slice the roll into 1-inch rounds and place them about 1 inch apart on the prepared baking sheets. Sprinkle the remaining filling on top of the rolls. Let the rolls rise for about 10 minutes, then bake them for about 20 minutes, or until golden brown.

CINNAMON ROLL FILLING

Stir together in a medium-size bowl:

> 1 cup unbleached flour
>
> 1 cup sugar or granulated sweetener of your choice
>
> 1 tablespoon ground cinnamon

Stir in:

> ½ cup raisins
>
> ½ cup canola or coconut oil
>
> 1 teaspoon salt

Pumpernickel Bread

This is a dark, moist, aromatic bread.

Combine in a large bowl and let rest for about 10 minutes, or until foamy:

   ¾ cup warm water (105 to 115 degrees F)

   2 tablespoons active dry yeast

   2 tablespoons molasses

Process in a blender until smooth and creamy:

   ½ pound firm regular tofu (at room temperature), mashed or crumbled

   ¾ cup warm water

Stir or beat the blended tofu into the foamy yeast mixture along with:

   6 tablespoons molasses

   ¼ cup canola, light olive, or coconut oil

Stir or beat in until the mixture starts to form a ball:

   3 cups dark rye flour

   3 cups whole wheat flour

   1 cup high-gluten bread flour

   2 tablespoons unsweetened cocoa powder

Turn the dough out on a floured board and knead until smooth. Place in a large oiled bowl, cover with a towel or plastic wrap, and let rise in a warm place for about 2 hours, or until about double in bulk. Punch down the dough, then knead and shape into 2 round or oblong loaves. Place the loaves on an oiled baking sheet, cover them with a towel, and let them rise for about 20 minutes, or until almost double in bulk.

   Preheat the oven to 450 degrees F. Bake the loaves for 20 minutes, then reduce the heat to 350 degrees F and bake for about 30 minutes longer, or until the loaves sound hollow when tapped on the bottom. Brush the tops with oil and cool on a wire rack.

Buckwheat Cakes

Combine in a large bowl:

   1 cup buckwheat flour

   1 cup unbleached or whole wheat pastry flour or cornmeal

   2 teaspoons baking powder

   ½ teaspoon salt

Process together in a blender until smooth and creamy:

   2½ cups water

   ½ pound soft regular tofu, mashed or crumbled

   2 tablespoons ground flaxseeds

   2 tablespoons canola oil

   2 tablespoons molasses or sorghum syrup

To make the batter, make a well in the dry ingredients and pour in the tofu mixture. Stir until the batter is smooth. It will look somewhat gooey.

   Heat a dry griddle over medium-high heat. Oil the heated griddle lightly and pour on about ¼ cup of batter for each pancake. When the tops of the pancakes bubble and look dry, flip them over and brown the other side. Serve hot with syrup or jam.

Rum Rolls

Serve these filled rolls for breakfast or brunch. They freeze and reheat well.

FOR THE DOUGH

Combine in a large bowl:

> ½ cup warm water (105 to 115 degrees F)
>
> ¼ cup sweetener of your choice
>
> 1 tablespoon active dry yeast

Let stand in a warm place for 5 to 10 minutes until foamy. Then stir in:

> 1 cup unbleached or whole wheat pastry flour

Let it stand for 5 to 10 minutes longer. Then stir in until well mixed:

> 4 to 5 cups unbleached or whole wheat pastry flour
>
> ¼ cup canola or coconut oil
>
> 1 teaspoon salt

Cover the dough with a towel or plastic wrap and let rise in a warm place until double in bulk, about 45 to 60 minutes. While the dough is rising, prepare the filling (recipe follows).

Preheat the oven to 350 degrees F, and oil 24 muffin cups. When the dough has doubled in bulk, punch it down and divide it in half. Roll each half into a ⅜-inch-thick rectangle on a floured surface. Spread each rectangle equally with the filling, then roll up it up jelly-roll style. Cut the rolls into 1-inch-thick slices. Place each slice in an oiled muffin cup. Cover and let rise until almost double in bulk, about 30 to 45 minutes. Bake for 15 to 20 minutes, until golden brown. Cool and brush with the frosting (recipe follows).

FOR THE FILLING

Beat together in a medium-size bowl:

> ½ pound soft tofu, mashed or crumbled
>
> ¾ cup brown sugar or sweetener of your choice
>
> 2 tablespoons canola or coconut oil
>
> 2 teaspoons rum extract
>
> ½ teaspoon salt

Place in a small bowl and pour boiling water over to cover:

> 1 cup raisins

Let the raisins soak for about 15 minutes until plumped, then drain and stir into the filling. Save the drained soaking water for the frosting (recipe follows).

FOR THE FROSTING

Beat together in a small bowl:

> 1 cup confectioners' sugar
>
> 2 to 3 tablespoons hot soaking water (from the raisins)
>
> 1 teaspoon rum extract

Brush or drizzle the frosting over the cooled rolls.

Blueberry Sally Lunn

Enjoy this mildly sweet breakfast cake packed with delicious, high-antioxidant blueberries.

Preheat the oven to 350 degrees F, and oil a 9 x 13-inch baking pan. Process together in a blender or food processor until smooth and creamy:

> 1 package (12.3 ounces) silken tofu, mashed or crumbled
>
> ½ cup sweetener of your choice
>
> ½ cup water
>
> 2 tablespoons ground flaxseeds
>
> 1 teaspoon vanilla extract

Combine in a large bowl:

> 2½ cups unbleached or whole wheat pastry flour
>
> 2½ teaspoons baking powder
>
> ½ teaspoon salt

Stir or beat into the flour mixture until evenly distributed:

> ¼ cup canola or coconut oil

Stir or beat the tofu mixture into the flour mixture just until it is evenly moistened. Fold in:

> 2 cups fresh or frozen blueberries

Pour and spread the batter into the prepared baking pan and bake for 30 to 35 minutes, until golden on top. Serve warm.

Tofu Pancakes

Combine in a large bowl:

> 2 cups unbleached or whole wheat pastry flour
>
> ½ cup cornmeal
>
> ¼ cup sweetener of your choice (if using a liquid sweetener, add it along with the soymilk)
>
> 2½ teaspoons baking powder
>
> 1 teaspoon salt

Stir together:

> 3 cups unsweetened soymilk
>
> ½ pound firm regular tofu, well crumbled
>
> 2 tablespoons canola oil
>
> 2 tablespoons ground flaxseeds

To make the batter, gently stir the soymilk mixture into the flour mixture with only a few strokes. The batter will be lumpy.

Heat a dry griddle over medium-high heat. Lightly oil the heated griddle and pour on about ¼ cup of batter for each pancake. Cook over medium-high heat until golden brown on each side. Serve with your favorite toppings.

Danish

This is one of our all-time family favorites. If you are using coconut oil, use one with little or no flavor. Danish is pictured on the opposite page.

FOR THE DOUGH

Combine in a large bowl:

- 1 cup warm water (105 to 115 degrees F)
- 1 tablespoon active dry yeast
- 1 tablespoon sweetener of your choice

Let stand for 5 to 10 minutes until foamy. Then stir or beat in:

- 2 cups unbleached or whole wheat pastry flour
- 3 tablespoons sweetener of your choice

Let rise until double in bulk. Combine in a small bowl or measuring cup:

- ½ cup canola or coconut oil
- ¼ cup sweetener of your choice
- 1 teaspoon salt

Add to the flour mixture, and mix it in with your hands.

Mix and knead in:

- 1½ cups unbleached or whole wheat pastry flour, more or less as needed (you will need 2½ cups flour if you used a liquid sweetener)

Knead the dough until it is smooth and soft but not sticky. Cover and let rise in an oiled bowl until double in bulk.

FOR THE TOFU FILLING

While the dough is rising, process in a blender or food processor until smooth and creamy:

- ¼ pound soft regular tofu, mashed or crumbled (½ cup)
- ½ cup water
- ¼ cup canola or coconut oil

Pour into a small saucepan and whisk in:

- ½ cup sweetener of your choice
- ¼ cup freshly squeezed lemon juice
- 2 tablespoons unbleached flour
- ½ teaspoon salt

PUTTING IT ALL TOGETHER

Cook over medium heat, stirring constantly until thickened. Remove from the heat let cool.

Preheat the oven to 350 degrees F, and generously oil 2 baking sheets.

Roll the dough out on a floured surface to ⅛ inch thick. It will be soft. Brush the dough with canola or coconut oil and cut it into 4-inch squares. Place 1 scant tablespoon of the cooled filling in the center of each square. If desired, place 1 scant tablespoon of cherry, blueberry, or poppy seed pie filling on top of the tofu filling.

Fold 2 opposite corners of the dough toward the middle and pinch them together. Take the remaining unfolded corners and curl them in toward the filling. Let the pastries rise for 5 minutes, then place them on the prepared baking sheets, leaving about 1 inch between the pastries. Bake for about 15 minutes, or until light golden brown. Brush with the tops with oil during the last 3 minutes of baking.

VARIATION

Prune Danish: Omit the tofu filling and place 1 scant tablespoon of Prune Filling (recipe follows) in the center of each square. Bring all 4 corners of each square toward the middle and pinch them together. Bake as directed.

PRUNE FILLING

Combine in a medium-size saucepan and simmer over medium-low heat until tender, about 10 to 15 minutes:

- 1 box (16 ounces) pitted prunes
- 2 cups water

Process the cooked prune mixture through a food mill or in a food processor until smooth with:

- 1½ tablespoons freshly squeezed lemon juice

Tofu French Toast

MAKES 8 SLICES

This egg-free breakfast treat contains no cholesterol and is always well received.

To make the batter, process in a blender or food processor until smooth and creamy:

> ¾ pound soft regular tofu, mashed or crumbled
>
> ½ cup water
>
> ¼ cup sweetener of your choice
>
> 1½ teaspoons ground cinnamon
>
> 1 teaspoon salt

Pour the batter into a shallow bowl, wide enough to hold a few slices of bread.

Dip slices of day-old whole grain or home-made bread into the batter, letting them soak briefly. Heat a large skillet or sauté pan over medium heat, brush it with oil, and brown the bread slices on both sides. Serve with maple syrup, jam, or jelly.

Danish

English Muffins

Combine in a large bowl and let stand for 10 minutes until foamy:

> 1 cup warm water (105 to 115 degrees F)
>
> 2 tablespoons sweetener of your choice
>
> 1 tablespoon active dry yeast

Process in a blender or food processor until smooth and creamy:

> ½ pound soft regular tofu, mashed or crumbled
>
> ½ cup warm water
>
> 1 teaspoon salt

Pour the tofu mixture into the foamy yeast mixture along with:

> 3 tablespoons canola or coconut oil

Stir in until smooth. Then stir in:

> 3½ cups unbleached or whole wheat pastry flour

Stir in to make a soft dough:

> 1 to 1½ cups unbleached flour

Knead the dough on a floured board for about 5 minutes, or until smooth. Place the dough in an oiled bowl, cover with a clean towel or plastic wrap, and let it rise until almost double in bulk, about 45 to 60 minutes.

Punch down the dough and divide it in half. Roll each half out to ½ inch thick on a flat surface generously sprinkled with cornmeal. Cut the dough into 3-inch circles and let rise for 10 minutes.

Heat a dry griddle or cast-iron skillet over low heat. Cook each round on the heated griddle for 5 to 8 minutes on each side, or until golden brown. Split the muffins in half and serve warm or toasted with your favorite toppings.

Flour Tortillas

There is nothing like a handmade tortilla hot off the griddle. Keep your tortillas hot by wrapping them in a towel or cloth. Flour Tortillas are pictured on page 132.

Combine in a large bowl:

> 4 cups unbleached or whole wheat flour
>
> 1 teaspoon salt

Process in a blender or food processor until smooth and creamy:

> 1¼ cups water
>
> ½ pound soft regular tofu, mashed or crumbled
>
> 2 tablespoons canola or coconut oil

Make a well in the flour mixture, pour in the tofu mixture, and stir until it starts to form a ball.

Knead into a smooth dough on a well-floured board. Divide the dough into 14 to 16 balls, each about 1½ inches in diameter. On a floured board, roll each ball out into an 8-inch circle.

Heat a dry griddle or *comal* over medium-high heat. Cook each tortilla on the heated surface for a few seconds on each side, or until it starts to puff up and has golden brown flecks on each side. Serve the tortillas wrapped in a cloth to keep them warm.

Hush Puppies

Hush Puppies are pictured on page 132.

Combine in a 3-quart bowl:

    2 cups unbleached or whole wheat pastry flour

    2 cups cornmeal

    4 teaspoons baking powder

    1¼ teaspoons salt

Stir in:

    ½ cup minced onion

Process in a blender until smooth and creamy:

    1¾ cups water

    ½ pound soft regular tofu, mashed or crumbled

Pour 1 inch of oil into a heavy skillet and heat it to 365 to 368 degrees F. To make the dough, stir the blended tofu into the flour mixture with a few strokes, just until moistened. Use 2 tablespoons of the dough to form logs or balls, and deep-fry them in the hot oil until browned all over. Serve plain or with mustard.

Sesame Tofu Crackers

Sesame Tofu Crackers are pictured on page 132.

Preheat the oven to 400 degrees F. Combine in a large bowl:

    3 cups unbleached or whole wheat pastry flour

    3 tablespoons sesame seeds

    1 teaspoon salt

    1 teaspoon baking powder

Process in a blender until smooth and creamy:

    ½ pound soft regular tofu, mashed or crumbled

    ½ cup olive, canola, or coconut oil

    ¼ cup water

Make a well in the middle of the flour mixture and pour in the tofu mixture. Stir or beat to make a soft dough, adding up to ¼ cup of water if necessary.

    Roll out the dough on a lightly floured board to ¹⁄₁₆ inch thick, and cut it into 3 x 14-inch strips. Place on a baking sheet and cut the strips diago-nally into 1-inch pieces, separating the pieces slightly. Bake for 12 to 15 minutes, or until golden brown. Watch them carefully so they don't burn. These crackers will keep for 2 to 3 months if stored in an airtight container at room tempera-ture, or for 6 months if stored in the freezer.

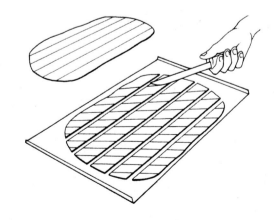

Banana Bread

This recipe works best when made with an electric mixer, but it can also be mixed by hand.

Preheat the oven to 350 degrees F, and oil a standard loaf pan. Process in a blender or food processor until smooth and creamy:

> 1 cup mashed ripe bananas
>
> ¾ cup mashed or crumbled soft regular tofu
>
> 2 tablespoons ground flaxseeds
>
> 1 teaspoon vanilla extract

Combine in a large bowl:

> 2 cups unbleached or whole wheat pastry flour
>
> ½ teaspoon baking powder
>
> ½ teaspoon baking soda
>
> ¼ teaspoon salt

Beat in until evenly distributed:

> ¼ cup canola or coconut oil

Beat in:

> 1 cup granulated sweetener of your choice

Beat in the blended tofu mixture. Then fold in:

> ¾ cup walnut pieces

Pour into the prepared loaf pan. Bake for about 1 hour, or until the middle springs back when lightly touched.

Noodles

Homemade noodles are a special treat. These are vegan noodles, using tofu in place of eggs. The spinach noodle variation makes a very special manicotti (see page 106). Noodles are pictured on the opposite page.

Place in a large bowl:

> 1¾ cups unbleached or semolina flour

Process in a blender or food processor until smooth and creamy:

> ½ pound soft regular tofu, mashed or crumbled
>
> 2 tablespoons olive oil (optional)
>
> ½ teaspoon salt

Pour the tofu mixture into the flour. Stir and knead by hand for about 10 minutes, or until it forms a smooth, soft dough. Alternatively, the dough may be mixed in a food processor or electric mixer with a dough hook.

Run the dough through a noodle machine or roll it out very thinly by hand on a floured surface and cut it into noodles. Let the noodles dry for 15 minutes; then boil them in salted water for about 5 minutes, or until tender.

VARIATION

Spinach Noodles: Wash, spin dry, and mince 1 cup of fresh spinach. Add it to the flour along with the tofu mixture. Proceed as directed.

Preheat the oven to 400 degrees F, and oil 12 muffin cups or cornbread molds. Combine in a large bowl:

2 cups cornmeal

2 cups unbleached or whole wheat pastry flour

4 teaspoons baking powder

2 teaspoons salt

Beat in until evenly distributed:

¼ cup light olive or canola oil

Process in a blender until smooth and creamy:

1½ cups water

½ pound soft regular tofu, mashed or crumbled

3 tablespoons sweetener of your choice

Stir the blended tofu into the cornmeal mixture with only a few strokes. Spoon into the prepared muffin cups or molds until they are about three-quarters full. Bake for 20 to 25 minutes, or until golden brown.

Noodles and Spinach Noodles

Chocolate Cheesecake with black cherry topping, page 156, and Cheesecake, page 155

swee

Sweets

7

Tofu excels at replacing eggs and dairy products in creamy sweets. Whether it is transformed into pie, pastry, cheesecake, pudding, topping, cake, cookies, bars, or ice cream, blended tofu takes on whatever flavor is added to it. Many of our family favorites are included here, especially ones for the holidays. For an everyday sweet, it's easy to make a simple fruit smoothie—just process soft or silken tofu in a blender with your favorite fresh or frozen fruit until it is smooth and creamy. Add sweetener to taste and a little soymilk to facilitate processing, if needed.

To make entertaining easier, many of the pies in this chapter can be made in advance. Chocolate-Peppermint Velvet Pie (page 151) or Tofu Ganache (page 153) are my favorite recipes to feed to those who are certain they don't like tofu—even though they may never have tried it. Pumpkin Pie (page 150) is a good choice to bring to the family holiday gathering, as it is sure to be well received. The sweeteners in these recipes can usually be varied according to your preference, but the amount may need to be adjusted depending on what you choose.

Black Bottom Pie and Gingerbread Cut-Out Cookies, page 175

Black Bottom Pie

This special pie has a double chocolate surprise—grated chocolate is spread over the cooled pie crust before the chocolate filling is poured into it.

Have ready:

> 1½ cups Sweet and Creamy Topping (page 161), chilled
>
> 1 (9-inch) graham cracker crust or regular pie crust, prebaked and cooled

Process in a food processor or blender until smooth and creamy:

> 1 pound firm regular tofu, mashed or crumbled
>
> 1½ cups confectioners' sugar
>
> 6 tablespoons unsweetened cocoa powder
>
> 1 teaspoon vanilla extract
>
> ¾ teaspoon soy sauce

Cover the bottom of the thoroughly cooled pie crust with:

> ½ ounce unsweetened or bittersweet baking chocolate, grated or shaved

Pour in the tofu mixture and spread it evenly in the pie crust. Chill for 8 to 12 hours, or until firm. Top the chilled pie with the Sweet and Creamy Topping and garnish with unsweetened or bittersweet chocolate shavings.

Coconut Tofu Cream Pie

Coconut milk imparts a creamy, pleasing texture to this pie. Microwave cooking will ensure a lump-free filling.

Have ready:

> 1 (8-inch) graham cracker pie crust, prebaked

Process together in a food processor until smooth and creamy:

> 1 can (14 ounces) coconut milk
>
> ¾ pound firm regular tofu, mashed or crumbled
>
> ½ cup sugar or sweetener of your choice
>
> 3 tablespoons cornstarch
>
> 1 teaspoon vanilla extract

Stir in:

> ½ cup unsweetened dried coconut flakes

Place in a 2-quart microwave-safe bowl or measuring cup and microwave on high for 4 minutes. Whisk until smooth and microwave for 4 minutes longer. Whisk until smooth and microwave for an additional 4 minutes. Whisk until smooth and pour into the pie crust. Spread with a spatula or gently shake back and forth to fill the crust evenly. Chill for several hours until firm.

Note: Alternatively, the pie filling can be cooked in a double boiler for 20 minutes. Stir constantly with a whisk to avoid lumps, and cook until thickened.

Orange-Vanilla Baked Custard

Preheat the oven to 400 degrees F, and generously oil and flour a 9-inch deep-dish pie pan. Process in a food processor or blender until smooth and creamy:

    2 pounds firm regular tofu, mashed
    or crumbled

    ⅔ cup frozen orange juice concentrate,
    thawed

    1 teaspoon vanilla extract

    ½ teaspoon salt

Combine in a small bowl:

    1 cup granulated sweetener of your choice

    ½ cup unbleached flour

    1 teaspoon baking powder

    ¼ teaspoon baking soda

Slowly add the flour mixture to the tofu mixture in the food processor or blender and process until smooth.

Pour into the prepared pie pan and bake for about 30 minutes, or until set and small cracks start to appear around the edges. Let the custard cool before slicing with a sharp, wet knife. Serve hot or cold. The custard will become firmer as it cools.

VARIATION

For a wheat-free custard, omit the flour, baking powder, and baking soda and add 3 tablespoons ground flaxseeds along with the sweetener.

Note: If you are processing the tofu in a blender, be sure to read Processing or Blending Tofu (page 4) before blending more than ½ pound of tofu at a time.

Pumpkin Pie

Surprise the family with this holiday favorite. They'll never know it's made with tofu.

Have ready:

    1 (9-inch) pie crust, unbaked

Preheat the oven to 350 degrees F. Process in a food processor or blender until smooth and creamy:

    1 can (16 ounces) pumpkin (2 cups)

    ¾ pound firm regular tofu, mashed or crumbled

    1 cup light brown sugar or granulated sweetener
    of your choice

    2 tablespoons molasses or sorghum syrup

    1½ teaspoons ground cinnamon

    1 teaspoon salt

    ¾ teaspoon ground ginger

    ½ teaspoon freshly grated nutmeg

Pour into the pie crust and bake for 1 hour, or until small cracks start to appear around the edges. Chill thoroughly. Serve with Sweet and Creamy Topping (page 161).

VARIATION

Sweet Potato Pie: Replace the pumpkin with about 1 pound (2 to 3 large) sweet potatoes, baked and mashed to equal 2 cups.

Chocolate-Peppermint Velvet Pie

This crowd-pleasing, no-bake dessert can be made a day ahead and chilled overnight for the best results. Alternatively, you can freeze it for a chilled treat that can be made several days or weeks in advance. More chocolate makes a richer and firmer pie.

Have ready:

> 1 (8-inch) graham cracker pie crust, prebaked

Process in a food processor until smooth and creamy:

> 1 pound firm regular tofu (at room temperature), mashed or crumbled
>
> ⅔ cup granulated sweetener of your choice
>
> 1 teaspoon peppermint extract

Place in a small microwave-safe bowl or measuring cup:

> 6 to 12 ounces semisweet chocolate chips

Warm the chips in a microwave oven on high power for about 1 minute, until they just start to melt. Stir the softened chips until all of them are melted and the mixture is smooth. Pour into the food processor with the tofu mixture and process until smooth, creamy, and thoroughly combined.

Pour into the crust and smooth it out with a spatula or shake carefully side to side to fill the crust evenly. Chill for 4 to 12 hours before serving.

VARIATIONS

Chocolate Almond or Vanilla Velvet Pie: Replace the peppermint extract with an equal amount of almond or vanilla extract.

Note: Alternatively, the chocolate chips may be melted in a double boiler over simmering water.

Frozen Peanut Butter Pie

This delicious and creamy frozen dessert is very easy to make.

Have ready:

> 1 (9-inch) pie crust, prebaked and cooled

Process in a food processor or blender until smooth and creamy:

> 1 pound soft regular tofu, mashed or crumbled
>
> ¾ cup creamy natural peanut butter
>
> ½ cup sweetener of your choice
>
> 1 teaspoon vanilla extract
>
> ⅛ teaspoon salt

Pour the tofu mixture into the cooled pie crust. Decorate the top with semisweet chocolate shavings or curls. Freeze the pie until solid. Let thaw for about 10 minutes before cutting and serving.

Plum Noodle Kugel

This is another family favorite modified to include tofu. This serves a crowd.

Preheat the oven to 350 degrees F, and oil a 9 x 13-inch baking pan. Combine in a large bowl:

> 1½ pounds firm regular tofu, mashed
>
> 1 pound egg-free flat semolina or whole wheat noodles, cooked and drained
>
> 1½ cups sugar or granulated sweetener of your choice
>
> 1½ cups unsweetened applesauce
>
> 1½ teaspoons ground cinnamon
>
> 1 can (3 pounds) plums, drained, pitted, and quartered

Spread the mixture evenly in the prepared baking pan. Combine in a small bowl:

> ¾ cup chopped nuts
>
> ¾ cup dried whole grain bread crumbs

Crumble the nut mixture evenly over the noodle mixture. Drizzle over the top:

> 3 tablespoons canola oil

Bake for 45 minutes. Serve hot or cold with Sweet and Creamy Topping (page 161).

VARIATION

Raisin Noodle Kugel: Omit the plums. Pour 2 cups boiling water over 1 cup dark raisins and let stand for about 15 minutes to plump the raisins. Drain the water and stir the raisins into the noodle mixture. Proceed as directed.

Note: This recipe can be cut in half and baked in a 9-inch square pan.

Banana Dessert

If you use plantains instead of bananas, this recipe will make twice as many servings.

Preheat the oven to 350 degrees F. Process in a food processor or blender until smooth and creamy and set aside:

> 1 pound soft regular tofu, mashed or crumbled
>
> 1¼ cups sugar or sweetener of your choice
>
> 3 tablespoons freshly squeezed lemon juice or distilled white vinegar
>
> 1½ teaspoons ground cinnamon
>
> ½ teaspoon salt

Cut in half lengthwise:

> 6 firm ripe bananas or ripe plantains

Heat in a large skillet or sauté pan:

> 2 tablespoons canola or coconut oil

Brown the banana halves on both sides in the heated oil over medium heat.

Arrange half of the bananas flat side up in an 8-inch square baking pan and cover them with half of the tofu mixture. Arrange the remaining bananas on top and cover them with the remaining tofu mixture. Bake for 20 to 30 minutes, or until the tofu mixture is lightly browned and set. Serve hot.

Note: If you are processing the tofu in a blender, be sure to read Processing or Blending Tofu (page 4) before blending more than ½ pound of tofu at a time.

Use this very rich, vegan ganache for cake fillings or toppings, or whenever ganache is called for in conventional recipes. You can also make creamy, melt-in-your-mouth truffles with this recipe. Alternatively, individual scoops can be mounded on gingersnaps or vanilla wafers for party treats.

Process in a food processor until smooth and creamy:

> ½ pound very firm regular tofu, mashed or crumbled
>
> ⅓ cup granulated fructose, confectioners' sugar, or other sweetener of your choice
>
> 1 teaspoon vanilla or almond extract

Place in a microwave-safe bowl or measuring cup:

> 1 cup semisweet or bittersweet chocolate chips

Warm the chips in a microwave oven on high power for about 1 minute, until they just start to melt. Stir the softened chips until all of them are melted and the mixture is smooth. Pour into the food processor with the tofu mixture and process until thoroughly mixed and smooth and creamy. For fillings or toppings, spread immediately and chill until firm.

VARIATIONS

For truffles: After the melted chocolate has been blended into the tofu mixture, stir in an optional ½ cup (or more) chopped candied ginger, dried cherries, chopped nuts, or shredded coconut. Chill until firm, then roll into balls using 1 tablespoon per ball. Roll the balls in unsweetened cocoa powder or dust the cocoa powder over them. Chill thoroughly before serving.

For individual servings: Chill the mixture until it becomes firm. Using a small cookie dough scoop or melon baller, scoop out 1 tablespoon at a time and press the domes onto the top of gingersnaps or vanilla wafers. Chill and dust with unsweetened cocoa powder before serving.

Note: Alternatively, the chocolate chips may be melted in a double boiler over simmering water.

Tofu Cheesecakes

Tofu cheesecakes can be made with a variety of flavorings and sweeteners. A medium-firm to firm tofu is best for making cheesecake. Be sure to read Processing or Blending Tofu (page 4) if you will be using a blender. If your tofu is very soft, try putting it between two towels with a weight on top of it for about 20 minutes to remove excess moisture. When a tofu cheesecake is done baking, it will appear slightly risen and will be firm on the surface with small cracks starting to appear around the edges. The middle may not have risen, but it will spring back to slight pressure from the touch of a finger and will have a dry, firm appearance.

Cheesecake

Cheesecake

Tofu cheesecakes are quick and easy to make. A quick topping is sliced seasonal fruit or berries, or you can use a can of pie filling spread or dropped in dollops on top. Cheesecake is pictured on pages 146 and 154, and on the front cover..

Have ready:

> 1 (10-inch) graham cracker pie crust, or 1 (10-inch) springform pan with a graham cracker crust pressed into it

Preheat the oven to 375 degrees F, and prebake the crust for 5 minutes. Process in a food processor or blender until smooth and creamy:

> 2 pounds firm regular tofu, mashed or crumbled
>
> 1½ cups sweetener of your choice
>
> ¼ cup freshly squeezed lemon juice
>
> 2 teaspoons vanilla extract
>
> Dash of salt

Pour into the cooled crust. Bake for about 40 minutes, or until it appears slightly risen and firm on the surface and small cracks start to appear around the edges. Chill thoroughly before serving. Serve topped with fresh fruit or a fruit topping. Sweet and Creamy Topping (page 161) can be spread on top of the cheesecake before arranging the fresh fruit topping, if desired.

Maple Tofu Cheesecake

Try topping this quick and easy cheesecake with additional maple syrup and chopped pecans.

Have ready:

> 1 (8-inch) pie crust, unbaked

Preheat the oven to 350 degrees F. Process in a food processor or blender until smooth and creamy:

> 1½ pounds firm regular tofu, mashed or crumbled
>
> 1⅓ cups maple syrup
>
> Dash of salt

Pour into the pie crust. Bake for 50 to 60 minutes, or until it appears slightly risen and firm on the surface and small cracks start to appear around the edges. Chill thoroughly before serving. Serve cold. If desired, drizzle with additional maple syrup and sprinkle with chopped pecans, and/or top with Sweet and Creamy Topping (page 161).

Chocolate Cheesecake

Chocolate Cheesecake is pictured on page 146.

Have ready:

> 1 (10-inch) springform pan with a graham cracker crust pressed into it

Preheat the oven to 375 degrees F, and prebake the crust for 5 minutes. Drain between 2 towels with a breadboard or similar weight on top for about 20 minutes to remove as much moisture as possible:

> 2½ pounds firm regular tofu

Process the tofu in a food processor or blender until smooth and creamy with:

> 2½ cups sugar or granulated sweetener of your choice

Melt in a double boiler over simmering water:

> 6 squares (1 ounce each) semisweet chocolate

Stir the melted chocolate into the tofu mixture along with:

> ½ cup sugar or sweetener of your choice
>
> 2 teaspoons vanilla extract
>
> 1 teaspoon almond extract
>
> Dash of salt

Pour into the cooled crust and bake for about 40 minutes, or until it appears slightly risen and firm on the surface and small cracks start to appear around the edges. Chill thoroughly before serving. Top with a fresh fruit glaze or cherry pie filling.

Note: For processing the tofu in a blender, process ½ pound of the drained tofu at a time along with ½ cup of the sugar until smooth and creamy. Stir all the batches together and proceed as directed.

Tofu Puddings and Topping

Tofu puddings need no cooking and are a creamy, delicious, high-protein, cholesterol-free treat. A firm or Japanese-style tofu is best for making puddings, since more liquid ingredients are usually added. Be sure to read Processing or Blending Tofu (page 4) before starting. Puddings should always be served chilled. Spoon them into individual serving dishes, or use them as fillings for a baked pie crust. For a creamy frozen dessert, pour any pudding recipe into a prebaked pie crust and freeze it. Let the pie thaw for 10 to 15 minutes before slicing and serving it.

If you are adding oil to any of the pudding recipes in this book, use one with a light flavor. Oil imparts a creamier consistency to the puddings and makes processing them in a blender easier, but the oil is not essential. For calorie counters, the puddings can be made without oil—you just may need to add a little soymilk to get the proper consistency. The sweetener can be replaced with stevia or xylitol, if you like. The Banana-Date Pudding (page 161) and Orange-Date Pudding (page 158) are sweetened only with the fruit in the recipe. The amount of the sweetener may need to be adjusted to taste depending on what you choose. Using liquid sweeteners will result in a softer, thinner pudding.

Carob Pudding, Strawberry Pudding, and Orange Pudding

Carob Pudding

Carob Pudding is pictured on page 157.

Process in a food processor or blender until smooth and creamy:

1½ pounds firm regular tofu, mashed or crumbled

⅔ cup unsweetened carob powder

½ cup sweetener of your choice

¼ cup oil (optional)

1 tablespoon vanilla extract

2 teaspoons freshly squeezed lemon juice

Dash of salt

Pour into individual serving dishes or a baked 8-inch pie crust. Chill until firm.

Orange-Date Pudding

This pudding is sweetened only with orange juice and dates.

Process in a food processor or blender until smooth and creamy:

1½ pounds firm regular tofu, mashed or crumbled

¾ cup pitted dates

½ cup frozen orange juice concentrate

¼ cup oil (optional)

1 teaspoon vanilla extract

Dash of salt

Pour into individual serving dishes or a baked 9-inch pie crust. Chill until firm.

Vanilla Pudding

Process in a food processor or blender until smooth and creamy:

1½ pounds firm regular tofu, mashed or crumbled

1 cup sweetener your of your choice

¼ cup oil (optional)

1 tablespoon vanilla extract

Dash of salt

Pour into individual serving dishes or a baked 9-inch pie crust. Chill until firm.

Orange Pudding

Orange Pudding is pictured on page 157.

Process in a food processor or blender until smooth and creamy:

- 1½ pounds firm regular tofu, mashed or crumbled
- ¾ cup sweetener of your choice
- ¾ cup frozen orange juice concentrate
- ¼ cup oil (optional)

- 1 teaspoon vanilla extract
- ⅛ teaspoon salt

Pour into individual serving dishes or a baked 9-inch pie crust. Chill until firm.

Banana Pudding

Process in a food processor or blender until smooth and creamy:

- 1½ pounds firm regular tofu, mashed or crumbled
- 3 ripe bananas
- ½ cup sweetener of your choice
- ¼ cup oil (optional)

- 1 tablespoon vanilla extract
- ¼ teaspoon salt

Pour into individual serving dishes or a baked 9-inch pie crust. Chill until firm.

Chocolate Pudding

Process in a food processor or blender until smooth and creamy:

- 1½ pounds firm regular tofu, mashed or crumbled
- 1¼ cups sugar or sweetener of your choice
- ⅓ cup unsweetened cocoa powder
- ¼ cup oil (optional)

- 1½ teaspoons vanilla extract
- ¼ teaspoon salt or soy sauce

Pour into individual serving dishes or a baked 9-inch pie crust. Chill until firm.

Apricot Whip or Pudding

Steam over boiling water until soft:

18 to 20 dried apricot halves (about ½ cup)

Process the softened apricots in a food processor or blender until smooth and creamy with:

1 pound firm regular tofu, mashed or crumbled

½ cup sweetener of your choice

¼ cup oil (optional)

⅛ teaspoon salt

Pour into individual serving dishes or a baked 8-inch pie crust. Chill until firm.

Strawberry Pudding

Strawberry Pudding is pictured on page 157.

Process in a food processor or blender until smooth and creamy:

¾ pound firm regular tofu, mashed or crumbled

1½ cups hulled ripe strawberries

½ cup sweetener of your choice

¼ cup oil (optional)

1 tablespoon freshly squeezed lemon juice

1 teaspoon vanilla extract

Dash of salt

Pour into individual serving dishes or a baked 8-inch pie crust. Chill until firm. Top with sliced strawberries.

Lemon Pudding

Process in a food processor or blender until smooth and creamy:

1 pound firm regular tofu, mashed or crumbled

⅔ cup sweetener of your choice

6 tablespoons freshly squeezed lemon juice

¼ cup oil (optional)

½ teaspoon vanilla extract

⅛ teaspoon salt

Pour into individual serving dishes or a baked 8-inch pie crust. Chill until firm.

Creamy Mango Pudding

Process in a food processor or blender until smooth and creamy:

2 large ripe mangoes, peeled and chopped (about 2 cups)

1 pound firm regular tofu, mashed or crumbled

¼ cup freshly squeezed lime juice

¼ cup sweetener of your choice

1 teaspoon vanilla extract (optional)

Pour into individual serving dishes or a baked 8-inch pie crust. Chill until firm.

Banana-Date Pudding

This pudding is sweetened only with fruit.

Process in a food processor or blender until smooth and creamy:

1 pound firm regular tofu, mashed or crumbled

2 ripe bananas

½ cup chopped pitted dates

¼ cup oil (optional)

2 tablespoons soymilk

2 teaspoons vanilla extract

1 teaspoon freshly squeezed lemon juice

¼ teaspoon salt

Pour into individual serving dishes or a baked 8-inch pie crust. Chill until firm.

Sweet and Creamy Topping

Serve this luscious topping as you would whipped cream. For the best flavor and texture, use only very fresh soft tofu.

Process in a food processor or blender until smooth and creamy:

½ pound soft to medium-soft regular tofu, mashed or crumbled

¼ cup canola or safflower oil (optional)

¼ cup confectioners' sugar or sweetener of your choice

1 teaspoon vanilla extract

½ teaspoon freshly squeezed lemon juice

⅛ teaspoon salt

Serve well chilled.

Cakes

All of the cakes in this book are vegan, free of eggs and dairy products. Adding tofu to cakes creates a moister crumb. For the best success, follow the directions exactly, always preheat the oven to the temperature specified in the recipe, and bake the cake immediately after mixing the batter. Try to avoid baking cakes that contain tofu on damp or rainy days to prevent them from becoming soggy.

*Blueberry-Lemon Cake
and Carrot Cake*

Blueberry-Lemon Cake

Blueberries and lemon are a natural combination in this light, egg-free cake. Blueberry Lemon Cake is pictured on page 162.

Preheat the oven to 350 degrees F, and oil a 6-cup Bundt pan. Process together in a food processor or blender until smooth and creamy:

> ½ pound firm regular tofu, mashed or crumbled
>
> ½ cup freshly squeezed lemon juice
>
> 2 tablespoons ground flaxseeds

Combine in a bowl with an electric mixer:

> 2½ cups unbleached, whole wheat pastry, or cake flour
>
> 1 teaspoon baking soda
>
> ½ teaspoon salt

Beat evenly into the flour mixture:

> ½ cup canola or coconut oil

Then beat in:

> 1¼ cups granulated sweetener of your choice

Pour in the tofu mixture and beat again just until blended. Fold in:

> 1 cup fresh or frozen blueberries

Spoon and spread the batter into the prepared Bundt pan and bake for about 50 minutes, or until the cake springs back from the gentle touch of a finger. Let the cake cool in the pan on a rack for 10 to 15 minutes. Loosen the edges of the cake from the pan with the flat side of a table knife, and then turn it out of the pan onto a rack to finish cooling. When the cake is cooled, place it on a serving platter and glaze with Lemon Glaze (recipe follows) or Creamy Lemon Glaze Topping (page 164).

Note: If you prefer to use a liquid sweetener, add 1 cup agave syrup or other liquid sweeter of your choice while processing the tofu. Lower the oven temperature to 325 degrees F and bake the cake for 5 to 10 minutes longer.

LEMON GLAZE

Stir together in a small bowl:

> 1½ cups confectioners' sugar
>
> 2 tablespoons freshly squeezed lemon juice

Drizzle over the top of the cooled cake.

Carrot Cake

Carrot Cake is pictured on page 162.

Preheat the oven to 350 degrees F, and oil and flour a 9 x 13-inch baking pan or a 12-cup Bundt pan. Process in a blender or food processor until smooth and creamy:

> ½ pound firm regular tofu, mashed or crumbled
>
> ¼ cup orange juice concentrate and ¼ cup water, or ½ cup orange juice
>
> 3 tablespoons ground flaxseeds
>
> 2 teaspoons vanilla extract

Mix in a large bowl with an electric mixer or by hand:

> 4 cups whole wheat pastry flour
>
> 2 teaspoons baking powder
>
> 2 teaspoons ground cinnamon
>
> 1 teaspoon baking soda
>
> 1 teaspoon salt
>
> ½ teaspoon ground allspice
>
> ¼ teaspoon freshly grated nutmeg

Beat or stir in until evenly distributed:

> ½ cup canola or coconut oil

Beat in:

> 2 cups turbinado sugar or granulated sweetener of your choice

Then beat in:

> 4½ to 5 cups grated carrots (about 1 pound)

Pour in the tofu mixture and beat until just moistened.

Fold in:

> ¾ cup chopped walnuts (optional)
>
> ¾ cup raisins (optional)

Pour and spread the batter into the prepared baking pan. Bake for 50 to 60 minutes, or until the cake springs back from the gentle touch of a finger. Cool in the pan on a rack. If the cake was baked in a Bundt pan, let it cool in the pan on a rack for 15 to 20 minutes, then loosen the edges of the cake from the pan with the flat side of a table knife, invert the pan, and slide the cake out onto a rack to finish cooling. When the cake is cool, top with Creamy Lemon Glaze Topping (recipe follows).

CREAMY LEMON GLAZE TOPPING

Process in a blender until smooth and creamy:

> ½ pound firm regular tofu, mashed or crumbled
>
> 3 tablespoons sweetener of your choice
>
> 1 tablespoon freshly squeezed lemon juice
>
> ¼ teaspoon salt

Creamy Filled Crumb Cake

This unique cake has a sweet crumbly topping and a creamy tofu filling.

Preheat the oven to 350 degrees F, and oil a 10-inch tube pan or 12-cup Bundt pan. Use 3 separate bowls to make the 3 layers.

FOR THE FIRST LAYER

Combine in a medium-size bowl until crumbly:

> 1 cup unbleached flour
>
> ½ cup brown sugar or granulated sweetener of your choice
>
> ½ cup chopped walnuts
>
> 2 tablespoons canola or coconut oil
>
> ½ teaspoon salt

Press into the bottom and sides of the prepared baking pan.

FOR THE SECOND LAYER

Process in a food processor or blender until smooth and creamy:

> 1 pound firm regular tofu, mashed or crumbled
>
> ½ cup sugar or granulated sweetener of your choice
>
> 2 tablespoons canola or coconut oil (optional)
>
> 2 tablespoons arrowroot or cornstarch
>
> 1 tablespoon vanilla extract
>
> ½ teaspoon salt

Spread the mixture carefully on top of the first layer.

FOR THE THIRD LAYER

Process in a food processor or blender until smooth and creamy:

> ½ pound firm regular tofu, mashed or crumbled
>
> 1 cup sugar or granulated sweetener of your choice
>
> 1 cup water
>
> ¼ cup canola or coconut oil
>
> 3 tablespoons freshly squeezed lemon juice

Combine in large bowl with an electric mixer or in a food processor:

> 2 cups unbleached flour
>
> ½ cup chopped walnuts
>
> 2 teaspoons baking powder
>
> ½ teaspoon baking soda
>
> ½ teaspoon salt
>
> ½ teaspoon ground cinnamon

Pour the tofu mixture into the flour mixture and beat, pulse, or stir it in until just blended with no lumps. Pour and spread the mixture over the second layer in the pan, being careful not to stir the second and third layers together.

Bake the cake for 40 to 45 minutes, or until it springs back from the gentle touch of a finger. Let it cool for 5 to 10 minutes in the pan on a rack. Then loosen the edges with the flat side of a table knife and turn the cake out onto a rack to cool. When completely cool, transfer the cake to a serving platter.

Strawberry Shortcake is pictured on the opposite page.

Have ready:

> 2 cups Sweet and Creamy Topping (page 161)
>
> 3 to 4 cups sliced or chopped fresh fruit or berries, sweetened to taste with sweetener of your choice

Preheat the oven to 450 degrees F, and oil an 11 x 17-inch baking sheet. Mix together in a bowl:

> 2 cups unbleached or whole wheat pastry flour
>
> $\frac{1}{3}$ cup sugar or granulated sweetener of your choice
>
> 2 teaspoons baking powder
>
> $\frac{1}{2}$ teaspoon salt

Cut in with a pastry blender or fork, or beat in with an electric mixer:

> $\frac{1}{3}$ cup canola or coconut oil

Process in a blender or food processor until smooth and creamy:

> $\frac{3}{4}$ cup water
>
> $\frac{1}{4}$ pound soft regular tofu, mashed or crumbled ($\frac{1}{2}$ cup)

Make a well in the flour mixture and pour the tofu mixture into it. Stir or beat just enough to make a smooth dough. Roll out to $\frac{1}{4}$ inch thick on a lightly floured surface. Cut into 24 rounds, about 3 inches in diameter, with a biscuit cutter. Place half the rounds on the prepared baking sheet. Brush the tops with canola or coconut oil. Place another round on top of each oiled one.

Bake the shortcakes for 15 minutes, or until golden. Cool on racks.

To serve, separate the top and bottom of each shortcake. Place the bottoms on plates, spoon on some Sweet and Creamy Topping, and then spoon on some of the sliced or chopped fresh fruit or berries. Place the tops of the shortcakes on the fruit and spoon on more topping and fruit.

Chocolate Pudding Cake

MAKES 9 SERVINGS

Preheat the oven to 350 degrees F, and oil a 9-inch square baking pan. Combine in a large bowl with an electric mixer:

    1¼ cups unbleached or whole wheat pastry flour
    ¾ cup sugar or granulated sweetener of your choice
    ¼ cup unsweetened cocoa powder
    1½ teaspoons baking powder
    ¼ teaspoon salt

Beat in:

    ¾ cup finely crumbled firm regular tofu
    ⅔ cup water

    ½ cup chopped walnuts or pecans
    3 tablespoons canola or coconut oil
    1 teaspoon vanilla extract

Pour into the prepared baking pan. Combine in a small bowl:

    1 cup sugar or granulated sweetener of your choice
    2 tablespoons unsweetened cocoa powder

Sprinkle the cocoa mixture over the top of the batter in the pan, and then pour on top:

    1 cup boiling water

Bake for 45 minutes. Serve hot, warm, or cold.

Strawberry Shortcake

Peach-Strawberry Upside-Down Cake

For an attractive presentation when the cake is inverted, try arranging the peach slices like flower petals around the strawberries in the bottom of the pan.

Preheat the oven to 350 degrees F. Combine in the bottom of a 9 x 13-inch baking pan:

¾ cup brown or turbinado sugar

¼ cup canola or coconut oil

Pat and spread the mixture evenly over the bottom of the pan.

Arrange on top:

1 pound frozen peaches, thawed, or 1 can (1 pound) sliced peaches, drained

16 to 20 fresh or frozen whole strawberries

Process together in a food processor or blender until smooth and creamy:

1 package (12.3 ounces) silken tofu, mashed or crumbled

1⅓ cups sugar or granulated sweetener of your choice

½ cup water

2 tablespoons ground flaxseeds

1 teaspoon vanilla extract

Combine in a large bowl:

2½ cups unbleached or whole wheat pastry flour

2½ teaspoons baking powder

½ teaspoon salt

Beat into the flour mixture with an electric mixer or by hand until evenly distributed:

⅓ cup canola or coconut oil

Pour the tofu mixture into the flour mixture and beat just until blended (about 10 seconds with an electric mixer).

Pour and spread the batter evenly over the arranged fruit without disturbing it. Bake for 30 to 35 minutes, or until golden and the cake springs back from the gentle touch of a finger.

Cookies and Bars

Individual sweets are always in demand. Tofu adds protein and helps keep these treats moist. Most of these recipes are old family favorites, updated with wholesome flours and less fat to make them more healthful.

Counterclockwise starting from the soymilk: Peanut Butter Cookies, Oatmeal Cookies, Carob Brownies, Date and Nut Bars, Chocolate Chip Bars, Chocolate Brownies, and Jam Dot Cookies

Jam Dot Cookies

These are a classic holiday cookies updated with the addition of tofu. They are pictured on page 169.

Have ready:

¼ cup unsweetened fruit jam of your choice

Preheat the oven to 350 degrees F, and oil 2 or 3 baking sheets. Process in a blender or food processor until smooth and creamy:

½ pound firm regular tofu, mashed or crumbled

½ cup walnuts

Pour the tofu mixture into a bowl and mix in with an electric mixer or by hand:

4 cups unbleached or whole wheat pastry flour

2 cups granulated fructose or granulated sweetener of your choice

½ cup canola or coconut oil

1 teaspoon salt

1 teaspoon baking soda

1 teaspoon vanilla extract

Roll into 1½-inch balls and place them on the prepared baking sheets. Press your thumb in the middle of each ball, leaving a depression. Bake for 10 minutes. Remove from the oven and drop ¼ teaspoon of the jam into each depression. Return the cookies to the oven and bake for 2 to 3 minutes longer. Cool on wire racks and store in covered containers with waxed paper between the layers of cookies.

Peanut Butter Cookies

Use only natural peanut butter for these cookies. If the peanut butter is salted, reduce the added salt. Peanut Butter Cookies are pictured on page 169.

Preheat the oven to 350 degrees F, and oil several baking sheets. Combine in a large bowl:

3 cups whole wheat pastry flour

1 teaspoon baking soda

½ teaspoon salt

Beat together in a separate large bowl with an electric mixer or by hand:

1 cup natural peanut butter

1 cup turbinado sugar or granulated sweetener of your choice

½ cup canola or coconut oil

1 teaspoon vanilla extract

Process in a blender or food processor until smooth and creamy:

¼ pound firm regular tofu, mashed or crumbled (½ cup)

½ cup agave nectar or liquid sweetener of your choice

Beat the tofu mixture into the peanut butter mixture. Then beat or stir it into the flour mixture until evenly combined. Form into 1-inch balls. Arrange the balls on the prepared baking sheets about 3 inches apart. Dip a fork into cold water and press it into the cookies to make a crisscross design. Bake the cookies for 10 to 12 minutes, until golden. Cool on a wire rack.

Chocolate Brownies

This was our best original brownie recipe, and it still holds up today. Chocolate Brownies are pictured on page 169.

Preheat the oven to 350 degrees F, and generously oil and flour a 10-inch square baking pan. Process in a blender or food processor until smooth and creamy:

> ½ pound soft regular tofu, mashed or crumbled
>
> ⅔ cup water
>
> ⅓ cup unbleached or whole wheat pastry flour

Pour into a small saucepan and cook over low heat, stirring constantly until thickened, taking care to avoid any lumps. Cool completely and pour into a medium-size bowl. Beat into the cooled mixture:

> 2 cups sugar or granulated sweetener of your choice
>
> 1 teaspoon salt
>
> 1 teaspoon vanilla extract

Mix together in a small bowl, and then stir into the tofu mixture:

> ¾ cup unsweetened cocoa powder
>
> ½ cup canola or coconut oil

Combine in a separate bowl:

> 1½ cups unbleached or whole wheat pastry flour
>
> 1 scant teaspoon baking powder

Stir the tofu mixture into the flour mixture, mixing well until there are no lumps. Pour and spread into the prepared baking pan. Bake for 25 minutes, or until a knife inserted in the middle comes out clean. Cut into 16 pieces.

VARIATION

For cakelike brownies, increase the baking powder to 2 teaspoons and bake for 20 minutes.

Soft Molasses Cookies

These moist, soft, egg-free cookies are classic favorites.

Preheat the oven to 350 degrees F, and oil an 11 x 17-inch baking sheet. Process in a blender or food processor until smooth and creamy:

> 1 cup molasses or sorghum syrup
>
> 1 cup canola or coconut oil
>
> ½ pound firm regular tofu, mashed or crumbled
>
> ½ cup turbinado sugar or dark granulated sweetener of your choice

Combine in a large bowl:

> 3½ to 4 cups unbleached or whole wheat pastry flour

> ½ teaspoon baking soda
>
> ¼ teaspoon salt

Pour the tofu mixture into the flour mixture and beat or stir until well combined. Drop by spoonfuls onto the prepared baking sheet. Bake for 10 to 12 minutes. Cool on a wire rack. Store in a tightly covered container to preserve the soft, moist texture of the cookies.

Oatmeal Cookies

Blended tofu combined with ground flaxseeds makes a good egg replacer for this kind of baking. Oatmeal Cookies are pictured on page 169.

Preheat the oven to 350 degrees F, and oil several baking sheets. Process in a blender or food processor until smooth and creamy:

> ½ pound soft tofu, mashed or crumbled
> 2 tablespoons ground flaxseeds
> 2 teaspoons vanilla extract

Combine in a large bowl with an electric mixer:

> 3 cups rolled oats
> 2½ cups unbleached or whole wheat pastry flour
> 1 teaspoon baking powder
> 1 teaspoon baking soda
> ½ teaspoon salt

Beat into the flour mixture until evenly distributed:

> ½ cup canola or coconut oil

Then beat in:

> 1½ cups turbinado sugar or granulated sweetener of your choice

Beat or stir in:

> ½ cup broken walnuts
> ½ cup raisins

Beat in the tofu mixture until well combined. Drop by 2 tablespoonfuls onto the prepared baking sheets, flatten each cookie to about ¼ inch thick, and bake for 15 to 17 minutes, until golden brown. Cool on a wire rack.

Chocolate Chip Bars

This is the bar version of chocolate chip cookies, with tofu and flaxseeds replacing the eggs. They are pictured on page 169.

Preheat the oven to 350 degrees F, and oil a 7 x 11-inch baking pan. Process together in a blender or food processor until smooth and creamy:

> ¼ pound firm regular tofu, mashed or crumbled (½ cup)
> ¼ cup water
> 2 tablespoons ground flaxseeds
> 1 teaspoon vanilla extract

Combine in a large bowl:

> 2 cups whole wheat pastry flour
> ½ teaspoon baking soda
> ½ teaspoon salt

Beat in:

> ⅓ cup canola or coconut oil

Then beat in:

> ¾ cup turbinado sugar or granulated sweetener of your choice
> ½ cup chocolate chips
> ½ cup chopped walnuts (optional)

Beat the tofu mixture into the flour mixture to make a crumbly dough. Press the dough into the prepared baking pan and bake for 20 to 25 minutes, or until lightly browned. Cool and cut into 12 bars.

Banana–Chocolate Chip Cookies

Here is a great option for using up ripe bananas.

Preheat the oven to 350 degrees F, and oil an 11 x 17-inch baking sheet. Process in a food processor or blender until smooth and creamy:

2 small ripe bananas

½ cup canola or coconut oil

½ cup brown sugar or granulated sweetener of your choice

¼ pound soft regular tofu, mashed or crumbled (½ cup)

1 teaspoon vanilla extract

Combine in a large bowl:

2 cups whole wheat pastry flour

½ teaspoon baking powder

½ teaspoon baking soda

Pour in the tofu mixture and beat with an electric mixer, or stir just until everything is evenly moistened. Fold in:

1 cup chocolate chips

½ cup chopped walnuts (optional)

Drop by tablespoonfuls onto the prepared baking sheet. Bake for 15 to 20 minutes, or until browned on the bottom.

Carob Brownies

Carob is actually a legume that contains a fair amount of protein, calcium, potassium, and phosphorus. Unlike chocolate, carob contains no caffeine and has a high percentage of natural sugars, so recipes that include it require less added sweetener for a sweet treat. Carob Brownies are pictured on page 173.

Preheat the oven to 350 degrees F, and oil a 7 x 11-inch or 9-inch square baking pan. Process in a blender or food processor until smooth and creamy:

½ pound soft regular tofu, mashed or crumbled

1 cup agave nectar or liquid sweetener of your choice

2 tablespoons ground flaxseeds

2 teaspoons vanilla extract

Combine in a large bowl with an electric mixer or by hand:

1⅔ cups whole wheat pastry flour

⅔ cup unsweetened carob powder

1 teaspoon baking powder

½ teaspoon salt

¼ teaspoon baking soda

Beat or stir in:

½ cup canola or coconut oil

½ cup chopped walnuts

Pour the tofu mixture into the flour mixture and beat or stir until smooth. Spread the batter evenly into the prepared baking pan. Bake for 25 to 30 minutes, or until it springs back from the gentle touch of a finger. Cool and cut into 16 pieces.

Whole Wheat Bittersweet Brownies

These cakelike brownies are for bittersweet chocolate lovers. If you like them sweeter, you can increase the sweetener (up to double the amount). Although they are made without eggs, they are very moist and even better the second day, if they last that long.

Preheat the oven to 350 degrees F, and oil an 8-inch round or square baking pan. Process in a blender or food processor until smooth and creamy:

> ½ pound firm regular tofu, mashed or crumbled
>
> ¾ cup water
>
> 3 tablespoons ground flaxseeds
>
> 1 teaspoon vanilla extract

Let the mixture stand and thicken while you beat together in a large bowl with an electric mixer:

> 1½ cups whole wheat pastry flour
>
> ½ cup unsweetened cocoa powder
>
> ½ teaspoon baking soda
>
> ½ teaspoon salt
>
> ½ teaspoon ground cinnamon (optional)

Beat in:

> ½ cup canola or coconut oil

Then beat in:

> ½ cup granulated fructose or granulated sweetener of your choice

Beat in the tofu mixture. Then fold in:

> ½ cup chopped pecans or walnuts (optional)
>
> ½ cup chocolate chips (optional)

Spread the batter into the prepared baking pan and bake for 25 to 30 minutes, or until it springs back from the gentle touch of a finger. Cool thoroughly before cutting into 12 pieces.

Pecan-Coconut Bars

Preheat the oven to 350 degrees F, and oil a 9-inch square baking pan. Combine in a large bowl with an electric beater:

> ¼ pound mashed or crumbled soft tofu (½ cup)
>
> ⅓ cup canola or coconut oil
>
> 2 tablespoons freshly squeezed lemon juice
>
> 1 teaspoon salt

Beat in:

> 1½ cups unbleached or whole wheat pastry flour
>
> 1 cup brown sugar, packed, or granulated sweetener of your choice
>
> ⅔ cup dried unsweetened coconut
>
> ½ cup rolled oats
>
> 1 teaspoon baking powder
>
> 1 teaspoon vanilla extract

Fold in:

> ½ cup coarsely chopped pecans

Pour into the prepared baking pan. Bake for 25 to 30 minutes, or until golden brown. Cool and cut into 12 bars.

Tofu Fudge Chews

These cookies keep well in an airtight container. They have a moist, chewy center with a crisp, sugar-coated exterior. Tofu Fudge Chews are pictured on page 169.

Preheat the oven to 350 degrees F, and lightly oil several baking sheets. Process in a blender or food processor until smooth and creamy:

    ½ pound firm regular tofu, mashed or crumbled
    ½ cup canola or coconut oil

Pour the tofu mixture into a large bowl, then beat in with an electric mixer or by hand:

    1½ cups sugar or granulated sweetener of your choice
    ½ cup unsweetened cocoa powder
    1 tablespoon vanilla extract (optional)
    1 tablespoon water or unsweetened soymilk

Combine in another bowl:

    3 cups unbleached or whole wheat pastry flour
    1 teaspoon baking soda
    1 teaspoon salt

Add the flour mixture to the tofu mixture and beat or stir until well combined. The dough should be fairly stiff. Roll into 48 (1½-inch) balls.

Place in a saucer or small plate:

    ½ cup sugar

Roll the balls in the sugar until they are coated all over, then place them on the prepared baking sheets 1 inch apart. Bake for 12 to 15 minutes. Cool on a wire rack.

Gingerbread Cut-Out Cookies

These are a holiday favorite for decorating and giving; see some examples on page 148.

Process in a food processor or mixer until smooth and creamy:

    1 cup sorghum syrup or molasses
    ½ pound firm regular tofu, mashed or crumbled
    ¼ cup canola or coconut oil

Combine in a large bowl:

    3½ cups unbleached or whole wheat pastry flour
    1 tablespoon ground ginger
    1 teaspoon baking soda
    1 teaspoon ground cinnamon
    ½ teaspoon salt
    ¼ teaspoon ground allspice
    ⅛ teaspoon ground cloves
    ⅛ teaspoon freshly grated nutmeg

Pour the tofu mixture into the flour mixture and stir or beat with an electric mixer just until combined. Do not overmix the dough or the cookies will be tough. If you are mixing with a spoon, you may have to use your hands to mix the last part. Chill the dough for 8 to 12 hours.

Preheat the oven to 350 degrees F, and oil several baking sheets. Roll out the dough on a lightly floured surface to ⅛ to ¼ inch thick. Cut into desired shapes with cookie cutters and arrange on the prepared baking sheets. Bake for about 8 minutes. Cool on a wire rack. Decorate as desired.

Date and Nut Bars are pictured on page 169.

Preheat the oven to 375 degrees F, and oil a 7 x 11-inch baking pan. Cook in a small saucepan over low heat until dissolved and thickened (about 15 minutes), then set aside to cool:

> 1½ cups chopped pitted dates
>
> 1½ cups water

Process in a blender or food processor until smooth and creamy:

> ¾ cup agave nectar or liquid sweetener of your choice
>
> ¼ pound soft regular tofu, mashed or crumbled (½ cup)
>
> 2 tablespoons ground flaxseeds

Combine in a large bowl with an electric mixer:

> 2 cups unbleached or whole wheat pastry flour
>
> 1½ cups rolled oats

> 1 cup chopped nuts (almonds, pecans, walnuts, or peanuts)
>
> 1 teaspoon salt
>
> ¾ teaspoon baking soda

Beat into the flour mixture until evenly distributed:

> ⅓ cup canola or coconut oil

Beat in the tofu mixture, mixing just until everything is evenly moistened. Press three-quarters of the dough into the prepared baking pan. Spread the cooled date mixture evenly over the dough. Drop small pieces of the remaining dough over the top of the date filling. Bake for 15 to 20 minutes, until golden. Cool and cut into 16 to 24 bars.

Note: For a crunchier bar, replace the agave nectar with 1 cup turbinado or brown sugar.

Ice Cream

Tofu ice cream has a unique creamy texture. Serve it as you would any ice cream—in a bowl, in a cone, on pie à la mode, or in a banana split. Put it between graham crackers and then freeze it for an ice cream sandwich, or spread it in a cooled, prebaked pie crust and freeze it for an ice cream pie. Use it between layers of cake and then freeze it to make an ice cream cake.

Use a light-flavored oil like canola for these ice creams. For fewer calories and less fat, tofu ice creams can be made without oil, but they will have more ice crystals and a less creamy texture. These recipes are meant for the larger hand-cranked or electric ice cream machines that will hold up to 14 cups of mix. Adjust the ingredient amounts for smaller home machines or simply process the mixtures in smaller batches. The amount of sweetener may need to be adjusted depending on what type you choose.

Mocha Tofu Ice Cream, page 179

Strawberry Tofu Ice Cream

MAKES 25 (½-CUP) SERVINGS

Process in a blender in 4 equal batches until smooth and creamy:

  2 pounds soft regular tofu, mashed or crumbled

  2 packages (20 ounces each) frozen unsweetened strawberries

  2 cups sugar or sweetener of your choice

  1⅓ cups unsweetened soymilk

  1⅓ cups canola oil

  ¼ cup freshly squeezed lemon juice

  2 tablespoons vanilla extract

  ¼ teaspoon salt

Freeze in a hand-operated or electric ice cream maker according to the manufacturer's directions.

Pineapple Tofu Ice Cream

MAKES 26 (½-CUP) SERVINGS

Process in a blender in 4 equal batches until smooth and creamy:

  2 pounds soft regular tofu, mashed or crumbled

  2 cans (20 ounces each) unsweetened crushed pineapple with syrup (set aside ⅔ cup drained crushed pineapple to stir in right before freezing)

  2 cups sugar or sweetener of your choice

  1⅓ cups unsweetened soymilk

  1⅓ cups canola oil

  ¼ cup freshly squeezed lemon juice

  2 tablespoons vanilla extract

  ¼ teaspoon salt

Stir in the reserved pineapple. Freeze in a hand-operated or electric ice cream maker according to the manufacturer's directions.

Carob Tofu Ice Cream

MAKES 18 (½-CUP) SERVINGS

Process in a blender in 4 equal batches until smooth and creamy:

  2 pounds soft regular tofu, mashed or crumbled

  2 cups unsweetened soymilk

  1 cup canola oil

  1 cup sweetener of your choice

  6 tablespoons unsweetened carob powder

  3 tablespoons vanilla extract

  ¼ teaspoon salt

Freeze in a hand-operated or electric ice cream maker according to the manufacturer's directions.

Chocolate Tofu Ice Cream

Process in a blender in 4 equal batches until smooth and creamy:

- 2 pounds soft regular tofu, mashed or crumbled
- 2 cups sugar or sweetener of your choice
- 2 cups unsweetened soymilk
- 1 cup canola oil
- ½ cup unsweetened cocoa powder
- ¼ teaspoon salt

Freeze in a hand-operated or electric ice cream maker according to the manufacturer's directions.

VARIATION

Mocha Tofu Ice Cream: Add 2 tablespoons of instant coffee granules to the mix prior to blending.

Strawberry Tofu Ice Cream, Pineapple Tofu Ice Cream, and Chocolate Tofu Ice Cream

Banana Tofu Ice Cream

MAKES 16 (½-CUP) SERVINGS

Process in a blender in 4 equal batches until smooth and creamy:

- 1 pound soft regular tofu, mashed or crumbled
- 5 ripe bananas
- 2 cups unsweetened soymilk
- ¾ cup canola oil
- ⅔ cup sweetener of your choice
- 3 tablespoons vanilla extract
- ¼ teaspoon salt

Freeze in a hand-operated or electric ice cream maker according to the manufacturer's directions.

Peach Tofu Ice Cream

MAKES 26 (½-CUP) SERVINGS

Marinate together in the refrigerator for 1 hour:

- 8 medium-size ripe peaches, peeled and chopped
- 1 cup sugar or sweetener of your choice
- ½ cup freshly squeezed lemon juice

Combine with:

- 3 cups unsweetened soymilk
- 1½ pounds soft regular tofu, mashed or crumbled
- 1¼ cups sugar or sweetener of your choice
- 4 tablespoons vanilla extract
- ½ teaspoon salt

Blend in a blender in 4 equal batches until smooth and creamy. Freeze in a hand-operated or electric ice cream maker according to the manufacturer's directions.

Glossary of Special Ingredients

Agar: Also known as agar agar and kanten, this vegetarian seaweed gelatin is rich in minerals and fiber and has a very mild flavor. The firmness of a gel made with agar will vary depending on the acidity of the foods used with it and the potency of the agar used. Agar is available powdered, flaked, or in sticks; I find the powder the easiest form to use. Look for agar in natural food stores, Asian groceries, and online.

Agave nectar: This low-glycemic sweetener is sweeter than table sugar and is recognized by the FDA as diabetic friendly. The body absorbs agave nectar slowly, thus preventing spikes in blood sugar. The nectar or syrup is expressed from the heart of the agave plant (the same part used to make tequila), a desert succulent native to Mexico, then filtered and heated. It is thinner than honey and contains up to 90 percent fructose in its natural form. Generally, about three-quarter cup of agave nectar can replace one cup of sugar in a recipe; when substituting agave nectar for sugar, also use slightly less liquid in the recipe. Look for agave nectar in natural food stores and online.

Broccoli rabe: A cousin of broccoli, broccoli rabe, also known as rapini, has dark green leaves and unopened flower buds. It is somewhat bitter but mellows when cooked; it is popular in Italian and Asian cooking. Look for broccoli rabe in supermarkets, natural food stores, and specialty produce markets. You can also grow some in your garden.

Chia seeds and chia seed oil: One of the four main protein staples (the others are corn, beans, and amaranth) of the pre-Columbian Aztecs, chia seeds boast the highest omega-3 fatty acid content of any plant. Traditionally they were used as a compact energy source for long journeys, as well as a base for medicines and vivid paints. Like flaxseeds, chia seeds can be ground and mixed with water for use as a binder to replace eggs in vegan baked goods. Chia seeds do not need to be ground for their nutrients to be absorbed. Look for chia seeds and chia seed oil at natural food stores and online.

Dulse: This sea vegetable from the North Atlantic is rich in iron and other minerals and also is high in protein. Purple-red in color, dulse has a soft texture when cooked and a somewhat spicy flavor. It is available dried or powdered at natural foods stores and Asian markets and online.

Flaxseeds and flaxseed oil: These shiny, flat, golden or brown seeds and their oil contain an abundance of essential omega-3 fatty acids. When ground and mixed with liquid, flaxseeds can replace eggs as a binder in vegan baked goods. I use a coffee grinder to grind the seeds as needed, and I store the whole seeds in an airtight jar in the refrigerator. Flaxseed oil can be added to uncooked dressings, sauces, and dips for a boost of omega-3 essential fatty acids. Flaxseeds and flaxseed oil can be found in natural food stores and well-stocked supermarkets; they are also available from online retailers.

Granulated fructose: Fructose, or fruit sugar, is about twice as sweet as table sugar and metabolizes more slowly, helping to keep blood sugar levels stable. It comes either granulated or as a liquid. The recipes in this book call for the granulated type. Look for fructose in natural food stores, supermarkets, or online.

Hempseed oil: Always use hempseed oil raw, uncooked, to maintain its superfood nutritional qualities. Hempseed contains complete, easily digestible protein and the optimum ratio of the essential fatty acids omega-3 and omega-6. Look for hempseed oil in natural food stores and online.

Kombu: Also known as kelp, kombu is a large, leafy sea vegetable rich in iodine and amino acids. Traditionally it is used in Japan to make a soup stock that is rich in glutamic acid. The dried leaf is sold in packages; it can be cut into smaller strips and boiled in water. Kombu is also available as a powder to add a burst of the flavor of the sea to any dish. Kombu can be found in natural food stores, Asian markets, and online.

Light olive oil: Light olive oil does not have a strong olive flavor and is best for recipes that require a more neutral-tasting oil. It still has the same calories per serving as any oil. Look for light olive oil in supermarkets and natural food stores.

Mirin: A sweet, low-alcohol wine made from glutinous rice, mirin is essential to Japanese cooking. It can be found in Asian grocery stores and the international or specialty section of well-stocked supermarkets. It may also be ordered online.

Miso: Sometimes called bean paste, miso is a traditional Asian food that is cultured and fermented to produce a variety of robust flavors, aromas, colors, and concentrations. It is based on barley, rice, soybeans, or chickpeas, with the addition of a culture and salt. Ranging from sweet to savory, miso delivers full-bodied flavors like fine wines. In addition to its rich flavor, unpasteurized miso contains high-quality protein, beneficial enzymes, and friendly bacteria that aid digestion. High heat will destroy the beneficial enzymes in miso, so only add miso to soups and dishes after they have been removed from the heat source and just before serving. Miso is purported to help prevent cancer and assist the body in recovering from radiation and pollution. Miso can be found in the refrigerated section of natural food stores and Asian markets. For more information and recipes for miso, see *Miso Cookery,* also by Louise Hagler.

Quinoa: A staple of the ancient Incas, quinoa is a delicately flavored seed that contains complete protein and is rich in manganese. Related to the beet and chard families, quinoa is also a cousin of amaranth, one of the four protein staples of the Aztecs. It is quick cooking with a light and fluffy texture and expands three to four times its volume when cooked. Quinoa is easily digested and gluten free. Look for quinoa in natural food stores, in specialty sections of supermarkets, and online.

Shiitake mushrooms: These highly prized, flavorful Japanese forest mushrooms have a smooth, buttery texture when cooked. Shiitakes can be purchased either fresh or dried and can also be easily grown at home. They contain all eight essential amino acids in good proportions, plus a healthful blend of vitamins and minerals. Shiitakes can help reduce serum cholesterol and blood pressure, aid in the production of interferon and interleukin compounds to help strengthen the immune system, and produce fat-absorbing compounds to aid in weight reduction. Shiitake mushrooms can be found in natural food stores, Asian groceries, and online.

Sorghum syrup: Sorghum syrup, sometimes called sorghum molasses, is an amber-colored, mild, natural sweetener made by cooking down the juice squeezed from crushed sorghum cane, a plant that originated in Africa and has traveled the world. About eight gallons of juice yield one gallon of syrup, which is rich in calcium, iron, potassium, and phosphorous. If sorghum syrup crystallizes in the jar, heat the container in a microwave or place it in hot water until the syrup liquefies again. Look for sorghum syrup in natural food stores, well-stocked supermarkets, specialty food shops, and online.

Soymilk: Unsweetened soymilk was used in the development and testing of all the recipes in this book. Because so many different sweeteners and flavors are now added to commercial soymilks, it is important to check labels carefully. Look for soymilk with no added sweeteners in natural food stores and supermarkets and online.

Tahini: Tahini is typically made from hulled raw or lightly roasted sesame seeds that are ground into a paste. Tahini can also be made from unhulled sesame seed, though it will have a slightly bitter taste. Rich in calcium, with a sweet, nutty flavor, tahini is commonly used in Middle Eastern cuisines. Look for it in cans or jars in natural food stores, well-stocked supermarkets, and international markets.

Tempeh: A flavorful high-protein food, tempeh is a traditional staple from Indonesia made from whole soybeans. To make tempeh, a special culture (*Rhizopus oligosporus*) is added to prepared soybeans or combinations of beans and grains, then the mixture is incubated while a mycelium (an edible fungus) grows between the beans, holding them together in a cake and breaking down the amino acid in the soybeans for easier digestion. Tempeh can be found in the refrigerated or frozen section of natural food stores and well-stocked supermarkets.

Turbinado sugar: Turbinado is a natural cane sugar in the form of large, crunchy crystals. It is made by crystallizing evaporated cane juice, then spinning the crystals in a centrifuge or turbine (thus the name "turbinado"). Its golden brown color comes from the molasses retained in the cane juice. Turbinado sugar is a good replacement for brown sugar. Keep it in an airtight container, as it tends to absorb moisture and become brick hard. Turbinado sugar can be found in natural food stores, supermarkets, and online.

Wakame: A sweet, mild-flavored leafy sea vegetable, cooked wakame combines well with land vegetables. It is a classic addition to Japanese miso soup and is especially rich in calcium, with a good amount of B vitamins and some vitamin C. Look for wakame in natural food stores, Asian groceries, and online.

Index of Recipes

Recipe titles appear in *italic* typeface.

BOOK PUBLISHING COMPANY

since 1974—books that educate, inspire, and empower

To find your favorite vegetarian and soyfood products online, visit:
www.healthy-eating.com

Books from Louise Hagler

Tofu Quick & Easy
978-1-57067-112-8 • $12.95

Lighten Up! with Louise Hagler
978-1-57067-011-4 • $11.95

Soyfoods Cookery
978-1-57067-022-0 • $9.95

New Farm Vegetarian Cookbook
978-0-913990-60-5 • $10.95

Meatless Burgers
978-1-57067-087-9 • $9.95

Miso Cookery
978-1-57067-102-9 • $10.95

Purchase these vegetarian cookbooks from your local bookstore or natural foods store,
or you can buy them directly from:

Book Publishing Company • P.O. Box 99 • Summertown, TN 38483
1-800-695-2241

Please include $3.95 per book for shipping and handling.